D0392659

Bridge Made Easy

Book Three
How To Win More Tricks

by Caroline Sydnor

Published by
Devyn Press, Inc.
3600 Chamberlain Lane, Suite 206
Louisville, KY 40241
1-800-274-2221
Fax 502-426-2044

See the back cover for ordering information

Dedicated to Betty Stockvis

First Printing October 1981
Second Printing November 1986
Third Printing October 1991
Fourth Printing January 2000
Fifth Printing October 2007

ISBN 0-939460-81-5

THANK YOU!

Many friends helped me with my book. It's a pleasure to get to thank them.

Betty Stockvis, a favorite partner, checked and re-checked each chapter with a critical and loving eye, made many helpful suggestions, and did research. To her I dedicate *How To Win More Tricks*. It's fitting the title personifies her card-play.

Marian Wertz, a student, typed — sometimes re-typed — the whole manuscript, always with that smile!

Lenore Macen, a student, did the tedious typing for the camera copy. A new, magic machine ate her pages, then spit out forms ready for the press.

Five fellow teachers tested a trial run of this book in their classes for a year — Becky Levering in Baltimore, Md.; Nan Logwood in Fairfax, Va.; Dot Lewis at the Crystal City Bridge Centre in Arlington, Va.; Carole Stromberg in Fairfax, Va.; Louise Webb in Albuquerque, N. M.

My own students at the Army-Navy Country Club used the chapters as lessons as I wrote them, gave me new ideas, and encouraged me. They are a joy in my life.

Caroline

Foreword

Bridge is such a fascinating game that it can become the most important thing in your life — while you're playing. A little luck combined with a lot of skill will produce excitement, satisfaction, and stimulation. Bridge offers the opportunity for brilliance, for cooperation between partners, for psychological warfare against the opponents.

The author has caught this spirit in her book *How To Win More Tricks*. Sure, it's primarily a teaching book — but it's much more than that. Through an adroit selection of hands, Caroline has made the game come alive! She starts you thinking. Suddenly you begin to see possibilities that you never dreamed existed. Suddenly you find a way to make an opponent give you a trick that he was sure was his. Suddenly you discover you can make an opponent throw away the setting trick by applying a vise-like grip that aficionados call a squeeze.

If you have already absorbed the material in the author's first two books, you can become a *good* player by mastering this one. Read it slowly, making sure you understand everything on each page as you go. Plays that turn ordinary players into experts are clearly presented so that an average player can understand them and quickly add them to his repertoire. Just imagine the feeling you will experience the first time you endplay an opponent to make your contract because you counted the hand and *knew* where every card had to be. There's nothing like it!

Bridge players are going to be telling their friends about this book. Rubber bridge players who master it will find themselves winning more; even duplicate players will find tactics to strengthen their game.

Henry G. Francis, Editor
The *Contract Bridge Bulletin*

CONTENTS

I. IT PAYS TO PLAN AHEAD

Testing out his bridge lessons at a party, Yale graduate William Webster picked up this South hand:

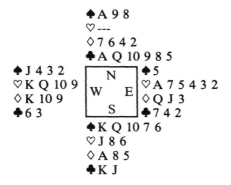

```
                  ♠ A 9 8
                  ♡ ---
                  ◇ 7 6 4 2
                  ♣ A Q 10 9 8 5
   ♠ J 4 3 2                      ♠ 5
   ♡ K Q 10 9      N              ♡ A 7 5 4 3 2
   ◇ K 10 9     W     E           ◇ Q J 3
   ♣ 6 3           S              ♣ 7 4 2
                  ♠ K Q 10 7 6
                  ♡ J 8 6
                  ◇ A 8 5
                  ♣ K J
```

North-South vulnerable

South	West	North	East
1 ♠	Pass	3 ♠	Pass
4 ♠	All Pass		

Opening lead, Heart King

"When dummy hit the table I counted thirteen winners. I'd never had a grand slam in my life. Looking at all those tricks boggled my mind!" handsome Will confessed. "I felt I'd been singled out by the gods for a special gift. I was so excited. I started taking tricks just as fast as I could. In fact, I played so fast . . . I botched it."

Will recounted how he ruffed the Heart lead in dummy, banged down the trump Ace and then the King. When East couldn't follow to the second round, Will had a problem but he didn't realize the magnitude of it.

Basking in the joy of taking tricks, he cashed the Spade Queen and then switched to collecting his Clubs. But West trumped in on the third round, took two Hearts, and eventually inherited a Diamond because . . . Will could no longer reach dummy's good Clubs. That meant down one, and the scorekeeper enscribed 100 in the East-West column.

One minute later Will figured out how he could make the hand — by simply giving West his trump Jack before starting Clubs. This way he'd lose only three tricks — a trump and two Hearts — and land his game.

"Then the scorekeeper would have written in *my* column!" Will exclaimed. "I'd get 120 for the tricks and 700 for the rubber. Added to the 100 I lost, I would have been 920 points richer for using my head at trick four."

Or, if Will had stopped to think at the very beginning, he might have found an even more lucrative play. His thoughts might have gone:

I have thirteen tricks available right now. Is there any possible danger? The answer is only if the opponents can get a trump trick. So, what is the trump story? Since we have eight, they have five. If theirs split 3-2, my thirteen tricks are ice cold. What if their trumps are 4-1? or 5-0?

With so many extra winners, suppose Will decides to make the safety play against the possibility of a bad trump break. At trick two he leads dummy's Spade 9, ducks in his hand, giving up a trick as a precaution against one defender holding J-x-x-x or J-x-x-x-x. West wins, but no matter what he returns Will has twelve golden tricks.

We can all join Will and profit from his loss. No esoteric card-play was needed to make his game. All he had to do was nurse his entry to dummy. He solved the puzzle all by himself a moment *after* the battle was lost. The secret to better bridge is *to take time to plan the play before touching that first card in dummy.*

Herein lies the greatest distance between the expert and the novice. All experts take time on every hand to plan ahead. Ely Culbertson, the whiz of the '30s, said it took him about 20 seconds. In a recent survey of 120 players at a tournament, the average time was 31 seconds. On many hands where there was no problem it was only 5 seconds. The record was set by a world champion — 1 minute 40 seconds.

During this study other players, as a courtesy, abstain from conversation while declarer is concentrating. This speeds up the process.

Some players say they feel hesitant "holding up the game". Your partner loves it because *you win more tricks*. Your opponents should be busy anyway, dreaming up potential lays-of-the-cards to defeat your contract.

When your study reveals you have enough tricks, take them and run! Many contracts have gone down the drain while the declarer finagled for an overtrick. Making extra tricks is attempted only when the contract is safe and there is no risk — as in Will's 4 Spade hand.

Many hands are easy to play and the tricks simply fall into your lap. Then there are tough ones. They're the challenge of the game. Often you have enough potential tricks to bring in your contract, yet the defenders have enough to set you. Thus a RACE develops to see which side can establish its tricks first. That's the reason it's urgent to plan.

There are four steps to guide you:

- Review the bidding
- Analyze the opening lead
- Count your tricks
- Explore ways to create more tricks

There is a mnemonic device to help you remember these. The first letter of each step spells RACE.

Review the Bidding

The first consideration is the information gleaned from the auction. When an opponent makes a bid start immediately estimating his distribution and his points — just as you do when your partner bids. The bidding sometimes helps you see through the backs of the opponents' cards, enabling you to play as though all hands were exposed.

When there is no adverse bidding, that tells you something, too. The outstanding face cards probably are divided. If one opponent has one missing Ace, the other often holds the other missing Ace. If there are two Queens outstanding and you find one on your left, the other is probably on your right.

<u>A</u>nalyze the Opening Lead

The opening lead is revealing. An honor card is usually the top of a sequence. A small card is probably from a broken suit; apply the Rule of Eleven* so you can win as economically as possible.

If you're playing No Trump and have only one stopper in the suit attacked, it may be wise to duck a round or two. Maybe one opponent will run out of cards in the suit. If this happens, communication between the defenders may be disrupted.

The lead may reveal you have a dangerous opponent you want to keep out of the lead. If you have a two-way finesse, take it toward the non-dangerous opponent.

<u>C</u>ount Winners or Losers

In general, you count winners at No Trump contracts. If you don't have enough, you look for ways to develop additional ones. At suit contracts you count losers. If you

---

* The Rule of Eleven is an infallible mathematical formula that operates when the opening lead is the fourth-best card in a suit. The formula enables the third player and the declarer to deduce immediately how many cards the other holds higher than the card led.

Subtract the spot on the card from 11. The answer gives the number of higher cards in the dummy, in the third hand, and in the declarer's hand. Since the third player can see how many he holds and how many dummy holds, he can tell how many declarer has. Similarly, the declarer sees his own and dummy's, so he can deduce how many the third player has.

have too many, you look for ways to dispose of some.

No Trump hands are simpler, so let's consider them first. Begin by counting your ready-made winners. Starting at one side of your hand, work your way across systematically suit by suit. Suppose Spades happen to be the suit nearest your thumb and you begin there. Study how your Spades mesh with dummy's Spades and add the Spade tricks available to you right now. Repeat with each suit.

Explore for Winners

In most hands declarer doesn't have enough tricks off the top. Suppose in a 3 No Trump contract you were a trick short, or worse, two or three tricks short! You must make a second study, suit by suit, searching for a way to develop winners. In No Trump contracts tricks may be created by:

- Taking a finesse
- Playing to drop an honor if the finesse seems hopeless
- Leading toward an honor
- Establishing a long suit
- Ducking
- Making an endplay
- Squeezing an opponent

Sometimes you have only one hope — maybe a finesse or establishing a long suit. If so, go for it. If Lady Luck is with you, you win. If not, you lose.

There are a few complicated hands with two or three choices where you weigh one play against the other, analyzing which is more likely to succeed. In choosing, be alert to danger signs:

- Do you have a dangerous opponent you want to keep out of the lead?
- Do you need to nurse an entry?
- Is there a suit you should unblock?
- Is there a timing problem?

With practice you can count and plan much more quickly than you can read this. Let's try counting and planning a hand together:

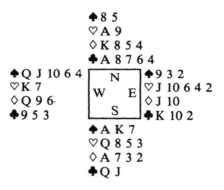

♠8 5
♡A 9
◇K 8 5 4
♣A 8 7 6 4

♠Q J 10 6 4
♡K 7
◇Q 9 6
♣9 5 3

♠9 3 2
♡J 10 6 4 2
◇J 10
♣K 10 2

♠A K 7
♡Q 8 5 3
◇A 7 3 2
♣Q J

South	West	North	East
1 NT	Pass	3 NT	All Pass

Opening lead, Spade Queen

Counting your winners you find only six — two Spades, one Heart, two Diamonds, and one Club. How can you develop three more?

Danger looms. If West has five Spades, he can establish three winners. You have only two stoppers and he is knocking out one now. You can afford to let the opponents regain the lead only once more. By then you must have nine ready-made tricks. Timing is the crux of the matter.

Exploring for tricks, you study each suit a second time, looking for possible ways to create additional winners. Spades — no chance for any more. Hearts — maybe one by leading toward your Queen, hoping East has the King. But you need three tricks, not one.

In Diamonds you hold eight cards and the opponents five. If theirs are divided 3-2, you can give up one round and create one winner. But you need three.

In Clubs you can establish one — the Queen or the Jack — by using one honor to knock out the King. You have seven Clubs and the opponents have six. If the suit is divided 3-3 (which is against the odds), you also could establish two small cards. Thus the Club suit could yield three additional tricks. It is the only chance you have. When you have only one chance, you take it.

Now that you have a plan, you're ready to play.

Duck the first Spade trick. It won't cost anything and it might help exhaust East's Spades. West continues his attack with the Spade Jack. You win the King.

You lay down the Club Queen, finessing. East wins the King, shoots back another Spade, and you take your Ace. The opponents' Spades are now established, but you're on lead and you aren't dead yet. You play the Club Jack, go to dummy with the Diamond King, and cash the Club Ace. When each opponent follows, establishing dummy's little Clubs, you are rewarded for your careful effort with nine tricks.

Let's try one more.

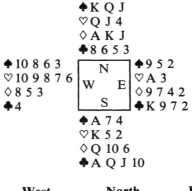

♠ K Q J
♡ Q J 4
◇ A K J
♣ 8 6 5 3

♠ 10 8 6 3
♡ 10 9 8 7 6
◇ 8 5 3
♣ 4

♠ 9 5 2
♡ A 3
◇ 9 7 4 2
♣ K 9 7 2

♠ A 7 4
♡ K 5 2
◇ Q 10 6
♣ A Q J 10

South	West	North	East
1 NT	Pass	6 NT	All Pass

Opening lead, Heart 10

With no adverse bidding to review, you begin by analyzing the lead. You see in a flash you have to lose the Heart Ace, but the suit itself is not a threat.

Counting winners, you find an unfortunate duplication of values. Some of your winners have to fall on the same trick with other winners. You have the four top honors in Spades but you can only get three tricks with them. The same is true of Diamonds.

Spades, three ready-made winners; Hearts, two; Diamonds, three; Clubs, three. Total, eleven tricks. Where can you find one more?

Exploring, you scour suit by suit. You discover the only chance is in Clubs. You can finesse for the King, and if it is on your right you can trap it and land your slam. You note there are five Clubs out against you and think how they are divided, 3-2, 4-1, or 5-0. Well, you can handle any of those so long as the King is in the East hand.

You have a plan and you are ready to travel.

You cover the Heart 10 with the Jack. East takes the Ace and continues Hearts. You carefully win in dummy to be in position to play Clubs because you will have to finesse several times if East happens to have a handful. You lead the Club 3, East plays low, you insert the 10. It wins!

Crossing back to dummy via the Diamond King, you lead another Club and finesse the Jack. Back to dummy with the Diamond Ace, you take a final finesse. Now you can claim your slam because all your cards are winners.

If West had the Club King, you'd go down. There's no shame in that. The shame is to go down when you could make your contract by planning.

Suppose on this hand you cashed all your sure winners first, using up the entries to dummy. Maybe you're dreaming the opponents will be careless and throw Clubs. Finally you get around to playing Clubs, but you can't get back to the board often enough to finesse Clubs three times. That would be a shame.

By planning ahead you saw you had to take the Club finesse, and you might have to take it several times, so you did it early while you had lots of entries.

Planning a Suit Contract

In a suit contract it is more expedient to count losers. There are fewer of them to add and they're easier to spot.

First decide which is to be the master hand. Declarer's hand is almost always the master hand because it is usually the longer in trumps. Using the same systematic approach of going from one suit to the next, *count the losers in the master hand.*

If you're in a 4 Spade contract with only three losers, go ahead and play. If you see four losers, make a second review to see where you can dispose of one. All the plays open to the declarer in a No Trump contract are available to you plus the advantage of the extra tricks you can create by using dummy's trumps to ruff. See if you can:

- Trump a loser in dummy
- Cross-ruff
- Take a quick discard on an extra top card
- Take a slow discard by establishing a long suit
- Throw a loser on a loser to build up a trick

Analyze the opening lead just as you would in a No Trump hand. If it is a small card, apply the Rule of Eleven. In addition, ask yourself, "Is it a singleton? a doubleton?" Are you threatened with a ruff?

Examine the trumps. How many do you have in your hand and dummy added together? How many do the opponents have? How are they divided?* Do you need to finesse or duck a round?

---

* In Chapter III we'll learn the Odd-Even Rule, a simple way to estimate the probabilities of how the outstanding cards are divided.

Here's an example of the way to analyze a suit contract:

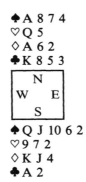

♠ A 8 7 4
♡ Q 5
♢ A 6 2
♣ K 8 5 3

♠ Q J 10 6 2
♡ 9 7 2
♢ K J 4
♣ A 2

North	East	South	West
1 ♣	Pass	1 ♠	Pass
2 ♠	Pass	4 ♠	All Pass

Opening lead, Club Queen

Analyzing the lead, you have two top winners and after that can trump Clubs in your hand. No problem.

Analyzing trumps, you have nine, they have four. The King is missing so you want to initiate trumps from your hand and finesse.

Counting losers in the master hand — one Spade, three Hearts, one Diamond, and no Clubs. Total, five losers.

Exploring for ways to eliminate losers, retrace your steps. In Spades you have a 50% chance to eliminate a loser with a finesse.

In Hearts, dummy has only two. You can trump a Heart loser in dummy if dummy still has a trump. With four trumps in dummy, this won't be a problem.

In Diamonds, you can lead from dummy toward your hand and finesse the Jack — a 50% chance to eliminate a loser.

New total: four losers. All you can do is take two finesses. If either wins you have your contract. If both lose, you're down. If both win, you have an overtrick.

Notice you did not bother with dummy's losers. For instance, dummy has two Club losers, but you didn't worry about them. That just slows down the whole process. What actually happens is they eventually fall on South's Spade winners.

See how quick that was! With experience it goes faster. Practice on this one:

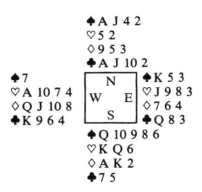

♠ A J 4 2
♡ 5 2
◇ 9 5 3
♣ A J 10 2

♠ 7
♡ A 10 7 4
◇ Q J 10 8
♣ K 9 6 4

♠ K 5 3
♡ J 9 8 3
◇ 7 6 4
♣ Q 8 3

♠ Q 10 9 8 6
♡ K Q 6
◇ A K 2
♣ 7 5

South	West	North	East
1 ♠	Pass	2 ♣	Pass
2 NT	Pass	3 ♠	Pass
4 ♠	All Pass		

Lead, Diamond Queen

Analyzing the lead, the Queen is top of an honor sequence. Although you have two stoppers, the opponents can establish a Diamond winner.

Studying trumps, you have nine and the opponents four. If they're split 2-2 or 3-1, all is well. You'll finesse for the King.

Counting losers, you find one Spade, two Hearts, one Diamond, and one Club. Total, five. Trying to eliminate two, you review each suit.

Spades, if the finesse loses there's nothing you can do — 50% chance.

Hearts, you can trump your third Heart in dummy — one loser eliminated. Another idea, if East has the Ace and you lead twice toward the K-Q-6, you can create a winner on which to drop a Diamond from dummy — 50% chance.

Clubs, a double finesse is available. If the King and Queen are divided you can set up a Club on which to throw the Diamond loser — 75% chance.

You decide to delay leading trumps and try the 75% play to establish a Club.

Winning the Diamond Ace, you lead a low Club, finessing the 10. East wins the Queen and plays another Diamond. You take the King and finesse again in Clubs. Your Jack wins! You play dummy's Club Ace and throw away your pesky Diamond loser. Feeling better?

Crossing to your hand by ruffing a Diamond, you lead the trump Queen. It loses to the King. East tries a low Heart and your Queen succumbs to West's Ace. West returns a Heart to your King. You pull trumps, ruff your little Heart in dummy, and the rest are yours. You take ten tricks, losing a Club, a Heart, and a Spade.

Suppose, instead, you had gone after trumps right away. When East wins the Spade King, he'll give chase with another Diamond. You win the Ace and faithfully pull trumps. However, when you eventually lose a Club trick, the defenders will also collect their Diamond trick. You still have to lose the Heart Ace, so you wind up going down one.

When you studied the whole hand at the very beginning, you discovered you had to set up Clubs before playing trumps. The timing of the Club play brought in the game.

You might like to plan this next one before reading what the real South did.

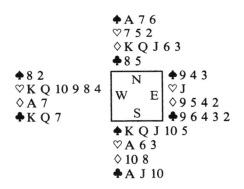

♠ A 7 6
♡ 7 5 2
◊ K Q J 6 3
♣ 8 5

♠ 8 2
♡ K Q 10 9 8 4
◊ A 7
♣ K Q 7

♠ 9 4 3
♡ J
◊ 9 5 4 2
♣ 9 6 4 3 2

♠ K Q J 10 5
♡ A 6 3
◊ 10 8
♣ A J 10

South	West	North	East
1 ♠	2 ♡	3 ◊	Pass
3 NT	Pass	4 ♠	All Pass

Opening lead, Heart King

Reviewing the bidding you decide West has five or six cards in the Heart suit for his 2-level overcall and probably holds most of the missing 15 points.

Analyzing the lead, you figure the King is the top of an honor sequence. East has a singleton or a doubleton. Analyzing trumps, you see the opponents have five and you hope they're split 3-2.

Counting losers you find none in Spades, two Hearts, one Diamond, two Clubs. Total, five.

Looking for ways to eliminate some of these, you see you can discard all your Club losers on dummy's Diamond winners if you can reach the Diamonds. The opponents can thwart you by ducking the first round and winning the second round. Then you can't get to dummy for the rest of your Diamond winners. Wait, you see a solution!

Winning the Heart Ace, you play the King of trumps and then the Queen of trumps. You are delighted when all follow. There's one more trump out but you abandon trumps for the moment because that trump Ace will guarantee an entry to dummy's Diamonds.

You lay down the Diamond 10 and everyone plays low. Then you continue another Diamond and West wins the Ace. He takes two Hearts and then plays the Club King. You win your Ace and play another Spade which extracts the last trump and, simultaneously, lands you in dummy. You collect two more Diamond winners on which you throw away Club losers.

Bringing home your game involved a well orchestrated plan — establishing a long suit in dummy and delaying the last trump lead to save an entry to the hand with the long suit.

TIP

When you count losers and can't find any way to make the contract, switch and count winners. Sometimes counting the other way helps you see a line of play you missed. It is better to count winners in certain trump contracts — (1) when you have a solid or nearly solid side suit; (2) when you have a pure crossruff and want to make your trumps separately; (3) when you're in a low-level contract.

Some players say counting winners is easier for them than counting losers. Count the way that's easier for you. The important thing is to estimate your liabilities or your assets before playing to trick one no matter how obvious the play appears to be. Failing to do so can be costly. The price once was life itself!

A High Penalty

The famous Bennett bridge murder occurred Sept. 29, 1929, and enlivened Kansas City for years. John S. Bennett, a personable and prosperous perfume salesman, and his wife, Myrtle, were playing rubber bridge with Charles and Mayme Hofman at a tenth of a cent a point, family against family. Just before midnight John dealt the fatal hand himself:

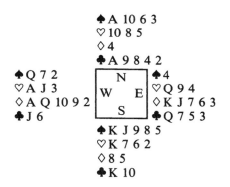

	South	West	North	East
	(John)	**(Charles)**	**(Myrtle)**	**(Mayme)**
	1 ♠	2 ◇	4 ♠	Pass
	Pass	Double	All Pass	

Opening lead, Diamond Ace

Hofman won the Diamond Ace, saw dummy's singleton, and switched to the Club Knave. Bennett took the King in his hand — the only correct play he made. He led the trump Jack. When Hofman didn't cover, declarer rose with dummy's Ace. He came off dummy with the trump 10. Mrs. Hofman showed out and Bennett took his King.

Next, Bennett trumped a Diamond in dummy, cashed the Club Ace, and led the Club 9. Mrs. Hofman played the Queen, Bennett trumped with the Spade 5, Hofman overtrumped with the Queen and cashed the Heart Ace. The Hofmans had their book.

Bennett won the next Heart and was stymied. Dummy had two good Clubs but he couldn't get over there. Confused, Bennett ran his trumps and had to go down two.

Myrtle goaded John about his poor play and John accused her of overbidding. One taunt led to another and another until Myrtle jumped up, dashed into the bedroom, grabbed the family pistol, came back and shot John dead.

Newspapers all over the world ran the story. Harpo Marx urged Alexander Woollcott, the raconteur of the day, to write an article about the episode and suggested the title, *Vulnerable*. Woollcott did write a humorous account but preferred his own headline, *Rude Bridge*.

During the trial some of the jurors became so intrigued with bridge they lost sight of the tragedy. Some learned to play between court sessions and asked for an expert to interpret the 4 Spade hand. The famous Ely Culbertson was summoned.

"Mr. Bennett overbid his hand," Culbertson announced. "Of that there can be no doubt, but even with this, so kind were the gods of distribution, that he might have saved his life had he played his cards a little better. He failed to make a plan."

Culbertson admired Mrs. Bennett's boost to 4 Spades and said he would have made the same bid himself.

The jury was swayed and brought in a verdict of "accidental death". Some months later a dazed insurance company had to pay double indemnity. Mrs. Bennett continued to play bridge but encountered some difficulty finding a partner.

On the fateful night Myrtle fired four shots. 'Twas said one was for each error John committed in the play. Can you find the four? (See Answers in back of book.)

Planning Drill

(1) The contract is 4 Hearts; West leads the Diamond 4.

♠ K Q 10 9 6
♡ 8 7 5 2
♢ 5   (a) Analyze the lead
♣ K Q 4   (b) Count the winners

                 (c) Count the losers in the master
                     hand
                 (d) Which count was quicker?
                 (e) What do you plan to do with
♠ J 7   the Diamond losers?
♡ K Q J 10 4   (f) Plan the play
♢ A 9 7 3
♣ J 5

(2) The contract is 4 Hearts; West leads the Club King.

♠ K 5
♡ Q J 3   (a) Analyze the lead
♢ 9 7 6 5 3   (b) How many losers in the
♣ 8 6 4   master hand?

                 (c) Plan the play

♠ A Q 4
♡ A K 10 9 6
♢ 4
♣ A 5 3 2

(3) The contract is 6 No Trump. East leads the Heart 10.

♠ A K   (Diamonds are split 3-2.)
♡ A 8
♢ A K 10 8 6 2 (a) Analyze the lead
♣ A 5 3   (b) Count your winners

                 (c) What problem do you
                     foresee?
                 (d) How can you create more
                     tricks?
♠ Q J 8 2   (e) Plan the play
♡ K J 4
♢ 7 3
♣ Q 9 6 2

1. Scheming for 12 Tricks

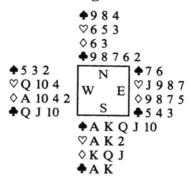

♠9 8 4
♡6 5 3
◇6 3
♣9 8 7 6 2

♠5 3 2　　　　　　　　　♠7 6
♡Q 10 4　　　　　　　　♡J 9 8 7
◇A 10 4 2　　　　　　　◇9 8 7 5
♣Q J 10　　　　　　　　♣5 4 3

♠A K Q J 10
♡A K 2
◇K Q J
♣A K

North deals
None vulnerable

North	East	South	West
Pass	Pass	2 ♠	Pass
2 NT	Pass	3 ♠	Pass
4 ♠	Pass	6 ♠	All Pass

Opening lead: Club Queen

There is a deck of cards that will deal quickly this identical hand, and all the other hands in *How To Win More Tricks.*

For the deck to work, the deal must rotate as it does in regular bridge. North deals hand 1, automatically receiving the cards printed in the North hand above. East deals hand 2, South hand 3, and West hand 4. Thus it follows throughout.

(To order cards see back cover.)

The late President Dwight D. Eisenhower loved bridge and had a regular game Saturdays at the White House. He advised a friend, "Play every hand as though bridge were a lifetime career. The result is more slams and fewer sets." Following that philosophy, South can make this hand.

With no adverse bidding and the lead carrying no threat, declarer began his study by counting the losers in the master hand. He was staring at two, a Diamond and a Heart. He couldn't hope to do anything about the Diamond Ace.

What about the Heart? Scrutinizing each suit in turn, he spawned a scheme to eliminate the Heart loser. Before reading on, see if you can discover his plan.

Winning the Club King, he laid down the Diamond King. West grabbed the Ace and shot back another Club honor. Declarer's Ace won. Pausing in his plan to take out a little insurance, declarer extracted two rounds of trumps. Then he changed gears.

South cashed the Diamond Queen, which absorbed dummy's last Diamond. When he laid down the Diamond Jack, he was able to discard one of dummy's Hearts. Next he played the Heart King and the Ace, breathing a sigh of relief when everybody followed. Now the coast was clear. He led his Heart deuce and trumped it with dummy's last Spade, the 9. Since declarer held all the higher trump spots, the 9 was a sure winner.

He ruffed a Club in his hand, extracted the last outstanding trump, and claimed the rest of the tricks to score his slam. President Eisenhower would have applauded the play.

Wasn't it risky to postpone the extraction of trumps so long? Yes! But if declarer pulls all the trumps immediately, defeat is certain. As he gathers in the opponents' trumps, he also removes all of dummy's. That means there's no Spade left to ruff the Heart loser.

Declarer's timing was brilliant. Observe what happens if he pulls two rounds of trumps before establishing Diamonds. When West wins the Diamond Ace, he can play his last trump to extract dummy's last trump. Then the slam goes kaput.

2. The Bidding Tells a Tale

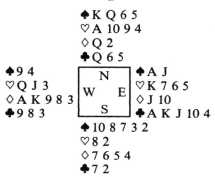

```
              ♠K Q 6 5
              ♡A 10 9 4
              ◇Q 2
              ♣Q 6 5
  ♠9 4                         ♠A J
  ♡Q J 3         N            ♡K 7 6 5
  ◇A K 9 8 3   W   E          ◇J 10
  ♣9 8 3         S            ♣A K J 10 4
              ♠10 8 7 3 2
              ♡8 2
              ◇7 6 5 4
              ♣7 2
```

East deals
North-South vulnerable

East	South	West	North
1 Club	Pass	1 ◇	Double
Redouble	1 ♠	2 ◇	Pass
2 NT	Pass	3 NT	

Opening lead, Spade 3

The bidding by the opponents often helps declarer find the winning line of play. Consider this hand where declarer's review of the bidding served as an invincible guide. Adding dummy's 10 points to his own 17, declarer calculated his adversaries held 13 points. For North's take-out double to make sense, North had to hold all those points.

Studying the opening lead also warned him of danger ahead. Declarer knew the opponents had nine Spades between them, probably divided 5-4, so they had four runnable Spade tricks whenever they regained the lead.

Counting tricks, East estimated five Club winners because he was confident North held the Queen and the finesse was going to succeed. Two Diamonds and one Spade totaled eight.

As he went exploring for one more, he realized he could set up a couple of Hearts or a couple of Diamonds.

However, whenever North got his Heart Ace or his Diamond Queen, North and South could cash four Spades and set him.

With these thoughts in mind, declarer captured the first trick with the Spade Ace, crossed to dummy with a Diamond to the King, and led the Club 9. He finessed and won. Next, another Club, again finessing, again winning. Now the Club King felled the Queen and declarer cashed two more Clubs.

At this point East had seven tricks stacked in front of him and dummy still had the Diamond Ace. He led the Diamond 10 and paused to reflect. Why take a finesse he was sure to lose? That's how it happened he ran up with dummy's Ace. Down crashed the Diamond Queen! This established three more Diamonds so declarer brought in eleven tricks.

Suppose declarer had paid no heed to the bidding and thoughtlessly finessed the Diamond. North would win the Queen, take four Spades and the Heart Ace, setting the contract two tricks. The bidding warned East — his only hope was to find the Queen doubleton — and guided him to the only feasible winning play.

3. Let the Opponents Help

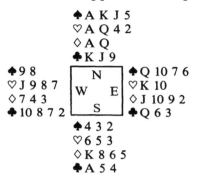

```
            ♠ A K J 5
            ♡ A Q 4 2
            ◇ A Q
            ♣ K J 9
♠ 9 8                        ♠ Q 10 7 6
♡ J 9 8 7      N             ♡ K 10
◇ 7 4 3     W     E          ◇ J 10 9 2
♣ 10 8 7 2     S             ♣ Q 6 3
            ♠ 4 3 2
            ♡ 6 5 3
            ◇ K 8 6 5
            ♣ A 5 4
```

South deals
East-West vulnerable

South	West	North	East
Pass	Pass	2 NT	Pass
3 NT	All Pass		

Opening lead, Diamond Jack

Analyzing the lead, declarer decided East probably held four or five Diamonds. Then he checked off eight ready-made winners — two Spades, one Heart, three Diamonds, and two Clubs. For his game-going trick he had a choice of three finesses — a Spade, a Heart, or a Club. Unfortunately, he had only one entry to dummy. Which finesse should he choose?

Looking a little further, thinking a little longer, he began to wonder what cards East held. What would East play back after his Diamonds were gone? A Spade, a Heart, or a Club? Any one of these leads would give declarer his ninth trick!

Thereupon, he won the Diamond Queen and cashed the Diamond Ace, noting that everyone followed. He entered dummy with a Club to the Ace. Now he led the Diamond King, throwing a little Heart from his hand. Both opponents followed so eleven Diamonds had fallen. Then he played dummy's last Diamond, discarding another Heart from his hand. East won the trick with his last Diamond.

East began to fidget and squirm. He was endplayed. He had no way out of his hand without presenting declarer with a free finesse. He had to lead away from his Spade Queen, his Heart King, or his Club Queen.

Helpless, he led the Spade 6. So North captured a trick with his Spade Jack, guaranteeing his game. But he wasn't through yet.

As he ran the Ace-King of Spades, of course he counted the Spades as they fell. On the third round West failed to follow, so East had the ranking Spade. This was the situation:

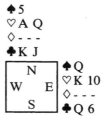

```
              ♠ 5
              ♡ A Q
              ◇ - - -
              ♣ K J
            ┌─────────┐   ♠ Q
            │    N    │   ♡ K 10
            │ W     E │   ◇ - - -
            │    S    │   ♣ Q 6
            └─────────┘
```

Declarer presented East with a second "present". He led the Spade 5 and East perforce won the Queen. Poor East, on lead again! He returned a Club. Declarer won the Jack, cashed the Club King, and took the Heart Ace. East got the last trick with the Heart King.

Declarer scored his game plus an overtrick and East, who began with five winners, ended up with only three. It Pays To Plan Ahead.

4. Keep Your Eye on the Ball

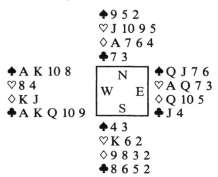

♠ 9 5 2
♡ J 10 9 5
♢ A 7 6 4
♣ 7 3

♠ A K 10 8
♡ 8 4
♢ K J
♣ A K Q 10 9

♠ Q J 7 6
♡ A Q 7 3
♢ Q 10 5
♣ J 4

♠ 4 3
♡ K 6 2
♢ 9 8 3 2
♣ 8 6 5 2

West deals
All vulnerable

West	North	East	South
1 ♣	Pass	1 ♡	Pass
2 ♠	Pass	4 ♠	Pass
5 ♣	Pass	5 ♡	Pass
6 ♠	All Pass		

Opening lead, Heart Jack

After East offered a jump raise in Spades, West became slam-minded, but he was worried about his worthless doubleton in Hearts. If partner had the Heart Ace he wanted to try a slam. If partner had the Diamond Ace and something like Q-J-x-x of Hearts, he didn't want to go.

That's why — after the trump suit was agreed on — West didn't use the Blackwood convention to ask East how many Aces he had. Instead, West cue-bid his lowest ranking Ace, saying 5 Clubs. This, in effect, asked East to cue-bid his lowest ranking Ace. East got the message; he called 5 Hearts to show the Heart Ace. Now West felt secure and contracted for the little slam. Then North kicked off with the Heart Jack.

Be grateful for tough opponents. They hold your feet to the fire and force you to play well.

If North had led any other suit, declarer would have an easy slam. There would be time to knock out the Diamond Ace and throw away a Heart loser on dummy's extra Diamond winner.

But now the Heart lead was establishing the opponents' Heart King before declarer could establish his Diamonds. The slam was in jeopardy.

Should he finesse the Heart Queen? Could North be leading from the King? A smart player might make such a daring play against a slam.

After careful study, he realized there was no way to dispose of his one Heart loser — but he discovered a way to get rid of all of dummy's Hearts.

That's why he refused the Heart finesse and won the Ace. He started after trumps and they fell in three rounds, so he still had one in dummy and one in his hand. He ran five Club winners, discarding all the rest of dummy's Hearts. Next, he played the Diamond King. North won the Ace but was helpless. He led a Heart but dummy, now void, trumped and declarer merrily marched in with his slam.

A lesser player who doesn't bother to stop and plan ahead would risk the Heart finesse. (He'd later explain, "I always finesse for a King.") When South grabs the King, he's going to send back a Diamond or a Club. Remembering the bidding (West opened with a Club), South easily hits on a Diamond. North takes the Ace and declarer is down before he even gets going!

II. MANAGING THE TRUMP SUIT

When you're declarer in a suit contract, let your first thought be, "Draw the opponents' trumps!" You have more than they have so you're in command. Take theirs away from them quick so they can't trump *your* winners! Of course you will have a few left to trump *their* winners. It's the way to win the most tricks and that's the fundamental principle of the game.

More hands are wrecked by the failure to extract trumps immediately than by any other declarer error. There's always the danger that an opponent has a short suit and can ruff one of your winners. A trick thus lost might cost the contract. It's a common fault of average players to start fiddling around with another suit. Suddenly someone ruffs in and declarer has to watch while Rome burns.

Holding the top trumps, lead them and keep on leading them, counting carefully until the opponents have no more. Then stop. Save all the rest in your hand and in dummy to win tricks separately by ruffing. If you lack the top honors but have the greater length, you still lead trumps until all the opponents' trumps are taken away.

Trump Tips

When you have eliminated all the opponents' trumps except one that's higher than any of yours, don't spend two trumps pulling one that's bound to take a trick anyway, unless you have a reason. It's wasteful. Here are some pertinent examples. South is in 4 Hearts and West begins by winning the King-Ace of Spades and continues the Queen of Spades.

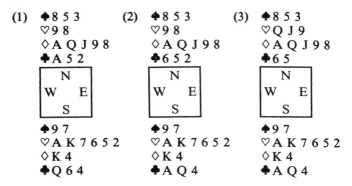

(1)   ♠8 5 3   (2)   ♠8 5 3   (3)   ♠8 5 3
       ♡9 8   ♡9 8   ♡Q J 9
       ◊A Q J 9 8   ◊A Q J 9 8   ◊A Q J 9 8
       ♣A 5 2   ♣6 5 2   ♣6 5

♠9 7   ♠9 7   ♠9 7
♡A K 7 6 5 2   ♡A K 7 6 5 2   ♡A K 7 6 5 2
◊K 4   ◊K 4   ◊K 4
♣Q 6 4   ♣A Q 4   ♣A Q 4

In Hand (1) declarer ruffs the third round of Spades, pulls two rounds of trumps with the Ace-King, all following. There is one trump outstanding and it's high, so declarer leaves it out and runs Diamonds until East trumps. Winning any return, declarer reaches dummy via the Club Ace and plays the rest of dummy's Diamonds, turning ten tricks.

Hand (2) is an exception to the rule because dummy has no entry outside the Diamond suit. After taking the Ace-King of Hearts, declarer plays another Heart to force out the Queen. This prevents an opponent from interrupting the run of the Diamond suit. If declarer plays Diamonds before forcing out the Heart Queen, East trumps, and declarer can't get back to the board for the other Diamond winners. Declarer spends two trumps corralling one for an excellent reason, as a wiser Will Webster taught us on page one.

Whenever your trumps are all high, extract all the adverse trumps even at the price of giving two to commandeer one. In Hand (3) East again has three Hearts but they are all little ones. Declarer plays three rounds of Hearts to take every trump East has even though on the second and third rounds he has to give two to pull one.

When there are two outstanding trumps and they're both higher than yours, there is a chance they are divided between the opposing hands. Be an optimist and lead trumps again hoping the two will crash on the same trick. In Hand (1) change the division of the trump suit:

(A)   ♡5

♡Q 7 3 [W N E S] ♡J 6 2

♡A K 10 9 8 4

(B)   ♡7 6 3

♡K [W N E S] ♡A Q J

♡10 9 8 5 4 2

In (A) declarer plays the Ace-King of trumps and continues a third round with the hope the Queen and Jack will fall together on the same trick. If declarer fails to continue Hearts, the opponents will probably win their honors separately, taking two tricks instead of one.

In (B) declarer holds the Ace-King of Spades instead of the Ace-King of Hearts and still reaches a 4 Heart contract. Missing the four top trumps it is urgent to lead trumps, hoping some honors will fall together on the same trick.

To Survive: Pull Trumps!

The importance of pulling trumps is illustrated in the following hand:

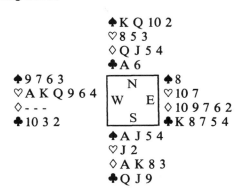

```
                      ♠K Q 10 2
                      ♡8 5 3
                      ◇Q J 5 4
                      ♣A 6
      ♠9 7 6 3                      ♠8
      ♡A K Q 9 6 4    ┌─────────┐   ♡10 7
      ◇- - -          │    N    │   ◇10 9 7 6 2
      ♣10 3 2         │ W     E │   ♣K 8 7 5 4
                      │    S    │
                      └─────────┘
                      ♠A J 5 4
                      ♡J 2
                      ◇A K 8 3
                      ♣Q J 9
```

North	East	South	West
1 ◇	Pass	1 ♠	2 ♡
2 ♠	Pass	4 ♠	All Pass

Opening lead, Heart King

West snaps up two Heart tricks and thereupon continues with the Heart Queen. South ruffs in his hand and surveys his prospects. He sees one more possible loser in Clubs.

Immediately he goes after trumps. On the second round he gets a nasty shock when East is unable to follow, revealing a 4-1 trump break. Nevertheless, he pulls all the trumps even though it takes two to get each one West has. He cannot risk losing a trick to a ruff. He takes four rounds of Spades, collects his four Diamonds, and cashes the Club Ace. (He can't afford the finesse.) That makes ten tricks and he's home.

Look back and see what happens if declarer fails to pull all the trumps and plays just one round of Diamonds. West surprises him by ruffing and the game is lost. Or, if declarer stops to try the Club finesse, which loses, East shoots out a Diamond for West to ruff. Either way declarer is doomed.

When To Delay Pulling Trumps

There are times, however, when declarer should postpone the pulling of trumps because there is important business he must attend to first. He delays only if it serves his purposes.

There are times when drawing even one round of trumps is fatal. On such occasions declarer should keep foremost in mind, "I'm going to draw trumps just as soon as I accomplish this one job."

Deciding whether to draw trumps immediately or to delay drawing trumps is the vital factor in the outcome of many contracts. The main reasons you might choose to delay are:

- To take a trump finesse
- To ruff a loser in dummy
- To crossruff
- To execute a dummy reversal
- To discard a loser
- To save an entry to dummy
- To save a "busy" trump

Let's look at each separately.

To Take a Trump Finesse. You have to cross to the other hand to finesse a missing trump honor. This one is easy.

(1)　♡ J 9 4

(2)　♡ 10 8 4

♡ A Q 10 7 2

♡ A Q J 9 2

Hearts are trumps and South wins trick one in his hand. It's to his advantage to finesse for the trump King so he delays pulling trumps until he can cross to the North hand.

After landing in dummy in example (1) he leads the Heart 9. If East has the King and holds it back, the 9 keeps the lead in dummy to repeat the finesse by leading the Jack. If East follows low again, a third finesse to the 10 can be taken. Likewise in example (2) declarer plays the Heart 8. If East plays a little card, declarer inserts the 2. This maintains the lead in dummy for a repeated finesse. Next comes the 10. Again, if East follows low, the 10 will hold the lead in dummy to finesse again.

The following deal is an example:

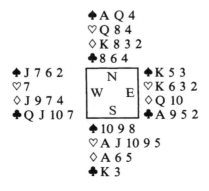

South	West	North	East
1 ♡	Pass	2 ◇	Pass
3 ◇	Pass	3 ♡	Pass
4 ♡	All Pass		

Opening lead, Club Queen

South faces five losers in the master hand — two Spades, a Heart, a Diamond, and a Club. His only hope is to try the single finesse in trumps and the double finesse in Spades.

East wins the first trick with the Club Ace and returns a Club to declarer's King. South is ready and anxious to lead trumps but he must start in dummy. Accordingly, he leads a Diamond to dummy's King and then plays dummy's Heart 8. When East follows low, declarer inserts his trump 5. When the 8 wins, declarer is ready to play dummy's Heart Queen and finesse again. The Queen wins and West fails to follow suit, revealing East began with four trumps. A third finesse is won by declarer's Heart 10 and the Ace brings down the King.

With trumps extracted declarer is ready to work on Spades. He leads the 10 from his hand and lets it ride. East wins the King and shoots back a Club. Declarer trumps with his last Heart, takes his Spade winners, and ekes out his contract with five trump tricks, two Spades, two Diamonds, and one Club.

The hand contains three key plays that occur over and over again in bridge: postponing the trump lead just long enough to cross to the opposite hand to finesse, playing a high trump to maintain the lead in the proper hand if the finesse succeeds, and taking the double finesse in Spades. It is a mathematical fact that a double finesse will find at least one of the two missing cards onside 75% of the time.

To Ruff a Loser in Dummy. When dummy holds a limited number of trumps and you need them for ruffing, often you can't afford to start extracting trumps because as you take the opponents' you also strip dummy's. However, the instant dummy's trumps have served their purpose, draw the opponents' trumps.

Whenever dummy has a void, a singleton, or a doubleton in a side suit, check to see if the shortness is of any use. When the closed hand holds losers in that suit, dummy's shortness is valuable.

Here's an illustration, a very important hand because of the rare contract:

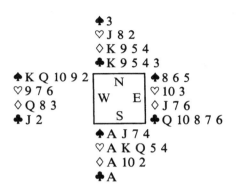

```
                    ♠ 3
                    ♡ J 8 2
                    ◇ K 9 5 4
                    ♣ K 9 5 4 3
    ♠ K Q 10 9 2                  ♠ 8 6 5
    ♡ 9 7 6           N           ♡ 10 3
    ◇ Q 8 3      W       E        ◇ J 7 6
    ♣ J 2            S            ♣ Q 10 8 7 6
                    ♠ A J 7 4
                    ♡ A K Q 5 4
                    ◇ A 10 2
                    ♣ A
```

South	**West**	**North**	**East**
2 ♡	Pass	3 ♡	Pass
4 NT	Pass	5 ♣	Pass
5 NT	Pass	6 ♡	Pass
7 ♡	All Pass		

Opening lead, Spade King

Declarer's reconnaissance reveals four losers in the master hand — three Spades and one Diamond. He can get rid of the Diamond loser on dummy's Club King (if he is careful to unblock the Club Ace), but what about those Spade losers? The only hope is to ruff them in dummy. He cannot afford the luxury of a single trump lead because all dummy's trumps are required to absorb the Spade losers.

Winning the Spade Ace, declarer plays a small Spade and trumps with dummy's Heart 2. Returning to his hand with the Club Ace, he plays another Spade and ruffs with dummy's Heart 8. Crossing back with the Diamond Ace, he leads his last Spade and trumps with dummy's Heart Jack.

All that accomplished, South begins to perk up. Coming off dummy with a low Club, he ruffs in his hand. Now, immediately — no monkeying around — he goes after trumps. The Ace-King-Queen of Hearts extract all the opposing trumps. Then a small Diamond to dummy's King lands him on the board to cash the Club King and throw away that Diamond loser. He takes all thirteen tricks.

Declarer utilized two fundamental principles of good card play. When ruffing he used dummy's lowest trumps first, saving the highest for the last round when East was most likely to be able to overruff. He also handled Clubs the safest way, ruffing the second round so he could lead trumps at the earliest possible moment. If he had cashed dummy's Club King and then ruffed a Club it would have been catastrophic. West was out of Clubs and ready to overruff. Walking a tight rope is an exhilarating experience when you don't fall off!

Every time you make a ruffing play, say a silent prayer you won't suffer an overruff. Declarer took the risk because it was the only chance to make the contract.

Whenever dummy has enough trumps to follow to trump leads and *then* take care of ruffing needs, pull trumps first. Suppose in this hand dummy held five Hearts. Declarer could afford two rounds of trumps first without draining dummy of its precious ruffing power. Suppose dummy had held four Hearts. Declarer could afford one round, saving the other three trumps for ruffs.

To Crossruff. When dummy is short in one suit and declarer short in another suit, a hand usually plays best as a crossruff. Never leading trumps, declarer strives to use all the trumps in his own hand and dummy's separately, ruffing first in one hand and then in the other. The technique is interesting.

First, prepare the crossruff. If you have a trick to lose in a suit to be ruffed, give it up right away.

Second, take your side-suit winners. A crossruff involves three suits — trumps, the suit being ruffed in dummy, and the suit being ruffed by declarer. In the fourth suit, cash your winners before you start crossruffing. Otherwise, as the crossruff proceeds, an opponent unable to follow suit throws cards in the fourth suit. When you belatedly lead your fourth-suit winners, the opponent will pounce on your trick with a trump.

Third, start by ruffing with low trumps, saving high trumps for later rounds when the opponents are more likely to over-trump.

If you can afford to lead trumps once, do; if you can't afford this precaution, don't. Remember, the time-honored defense against a crossruff is for the defenders to lead trumps at every opportunity. If declarer wants to make his trumps one at a time, the defenders want him to have to play two at a time. Therefore, if an opponent gains the lead, he'll try to shorten declarer by leading trumps.

Here's a crossruff that employs all these principles:

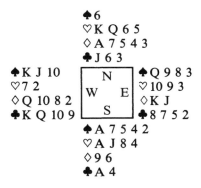

```
                    ♠ 6
                    ♡ K Q 6 5
                    ◊ A 7 5 4 3
                    ♣ J 6 3
    ♠ K J 10        ┌─────────┐    ♠ Q 9 8 3
    ♡ 7 2           │    N    │    ♡ 10 9 3
    ◊ Q 10 8 2      │ W     E │    ◊ K J
    ♣ K Q 10 9      │    S    │    ♣ 8 7 5 2
                    └─────────┘
                    ♠ A 7 5 4 2
                    ♡ A J 8 4
                    ◊ 9 6
                    ♣ A 4
```

South	West	North	East
1 ♠	Pass	2 ◊	Pass
2 ♡	Pass	4 ♡	All Pass

Opening lead, Club King

Declarer counts six losers in the master hand. The opening lead gives him an opportunity to set up the Jack of Clubs, which takes care of one loser, but he still has two too many. Then he sees the hand is tailor-made for a crossruff, trumping Spades in dummy and Diamonds in his hand.

The first priority is to set up the crossruff and he accomplishes this in an unusual way. He wins the Club King with his Ace and leads a Club. West takes his Queen.

Clever West, seeing the Spade singleton in dummy, suspects a crossruff and shoots back a trump. Declarer wins in dummy with the Heart Queen and lays down the Club Jack, discarding a Diamond from the closed hand. Now the crossruff is ready and the winners in the fourth suit (Clubs) have been cashed.

Declarer plays the Diamond Ace and ruffs a Diamond with his lowest trump; cashes the Spade Ace and ruffs a Spade with dummy's lowest trump; ruffs another Diamond, ruffs another Spade, ruffs a Diamond, and ruffs a Spade. That's eleven tricks — two Clubs, one Spade, one Diamond, and seven trump tricks.

Replay the hand without West's trump lead and watch South take twelve tricks because he gets one more trump trick. Replay it once more with declarer extracting trumps and watch him go down one!

To Execute a Dummy Reversal. One of the cardinal principles of good declarer play is to look for ways to use dummy's trumps to ruff losers but to avoid ruffing in the closed hand, saving declarer's long trumps for the important mission of extracting the opponents trumps.

In the "dummy reversal" the roles of the two hands are switched. Declarer's trumps are used for ruffing, and dummy's trumps are used to draw trumps. The dummy reversal is just as simple to execute as its opposite. The problem is to diagnose that the hand should be played in this backward manner.

How can you recognize a dummy reversal? By counting your tricks and looking for a way to take more. If the declarer in the next hand hadn't foreseen a dummy reversal, he would have gone down. Before reading on, try it yourself.

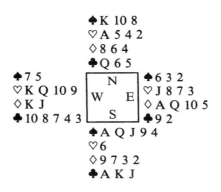

♠ K 10 8
♡ A 5 4 2
◇ 8 6 4
♣ Q 6 5

♠ 7 5
♡ K Q 10 9
◇ K J
♣ 10 8 7 4 3

♠ 6 3 2
♡ J 8 7 3
◇ A Q 10 5
♣ 9 2

♠ A Q J 9 4
♡ 6
◇ 9 7 3 2
♣ A K J

South	West	North	East
1 ♠	Pass	2 ♠	Pass
3 ♠	Pass	4 ♠	All Pass

Opening lead, Heart King

You find four Diamond losers in the master hand and can't find any place to dispose of them. Studying your puzzle, you try counting winners and see five Spade tricks, one Heart, and three Clubs — a total of nine. You probe for one more.

If the Diamonds split 3-3 you can establish a small Diamond, but finding that idyllic situation is rare. You look further.

Dummy has no short suit so you can't pick up a trick by ruffing in dummy. The only hand with a short suit is declarer's, which could ruff three Hearts. If you try that, you then could use dummy's trumps to pull the opponents'. This yields six Spade tricks instead of five — dummy's three plus three ruffs in your hand — and brings your total up to ten tricks.

This will work if the five adverse trumps divide 3-2, the normal split. This seems more likely to succeed than the Diamond play, and the odds worked out by mathematicians back this up.

Proceeding on this plan, you win the Heart Ace, continue a Heart, and trump with a Spade honor. The Spade 4 to dummy's 8 gets you back on the board to lead a third Heart, which you ruff with another Spade honor. You play the Spade 9 to dummy's 10 and happily observe everybody following suit because now there's only one trump outstanding. You play dummy's last Heart and ruff with South's last Spade.

Then, the Club Jack overtaken by the Queen lands you in dummy to lead dummy's last trump, the King, which draws the last outstanding Spade. Since the closed hand is out of trumps, it discards a Diamond loser. Next you win your Ace-King of Clubs, raking in ten tricks, and cheerfully concede the last three tricks to the opponents' high Diamonds.

You see, the execution isn't so tough. It's making the diagnosis that is difficult. Here are the conditions that existed to make the dummy reversal possible:

- Declarer's hand contained a short suit
- Dummy's trumps were high enough to extract the adverse trumps
- The outstanding trumps divided favorably.
- Dummy had enough entries.

A dummy reversal hinges on dummy entries. Notice the unblocking of South's big trumps to reserve low trumps to reach dummy. Declarer ruffs with honors, saving the 4 and 9 to enter dummy. Observe the importance of dummy's Club Queen. Without it, you can't even flirt with the idea because you can't get back to pull the last trump.

To Discard a Loser. Sometimes you postpone leading trumps to make a quick discard of a loser. An opponent has a big trump and you have to get rid of a loser before you let him in.

The following deal illustrates the point:

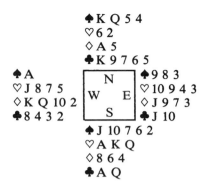

♠K Q 5 4			
♡6 2			
◇A 5			
♣K 9 7 6 5			

♠A   ♠9 8 3
♡J 8 7 5   ♡10 9 4 3
◇K Q 10 2   ◇J 9 7 3
♣8 4 3 2   ♣J 10

♠J 10 7 6 2
♡A K Q
◇8 6 4
♣A Q

South	West	North	East
1 ♠	Pass	3 ♠	Pass
4 ♣	Pass	4 ◇	Pass
6 ♠	All Pass		

Opening lead, Diamond King

Just a note about the auction. South was interested in a slam but was worried about Diamond losers. After a trump suit was agreed on, he decided it would be more illuminating to cue-bid Aces than to use the Blackwood Convention. His 4 Club bid showed the Club Ace; then North's 4 Diamond bid showed the Diamond Ace. As soon as South heard that call, he was ready for 6 Spades.

Now dummy comes down and the master hand holds three losers — a trump and two Diamonds. Since dummy has a doubleton Diamond, one of declarer's can be ruffed, but the other Diamond loser will scuttle the slam.

All is not lost yet. Declarer sees a place to pitch dummy's Diamond! Winning the Diamond Ace, he postpones leading trumps for a more important mission. He plays the Ace-King-Queen of Hearts and on the third round discards dummy's Diamond 5.

Then, immediately, he goes after trumps. West wins the Ace but can no longer get a Diamond and South easily coasts in with his slam. He captures any return, extracts trumps, and unblocks Clubs by cashing the Ace-Queen.

Then he ruffs a Diamond in dummy and leads the Club King to discard the other Diamond from the closed hand. Now he can claim.

It would have been short-sighted to lead trumps at trick two before jettisonning the Diamond. In bridge it pays to plan ahead!

Another example, more advanced, is this layout:

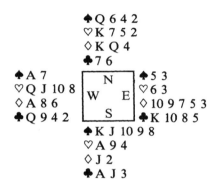

```
                   ♠ Q 6 4 2
                   ♡ K 7 5 2
                   ◇ K Q 4
                   ♣ 7 6
        ♠ A 7                    ♠ 5 3
        ♡ Q J 10 8    N          ♡ 6 3
        ◇ A 8 6    W     E       ◇ 10 9 7 5 3
        ♣ Q 9 4 2     S          ♣ K 10 8 5
                   ♠ K J 10 9 8
                   ♡ A 9 4
                   ◇ J 2
                   ♣ A J 3
```

South	West	North	East
1 ♠	Double	Redouble	2 ◇
Pass	Pass	2 ♠	Pass
3 ♠	Pass	4 ♠	All Pass

Opening lead, Heart Queen

Declarer's study shows a loser in each suit. (He has two Club losers but one, of course, can be ruffed.) There isn't anything he can do about the Spade Ace or the Diamond Ace, so he has to do something about the Heart loser or the Club loser to salvage his game.

Reviewing the hand suit by suit, he discovers an extra Diamond winner on which he can discard a Heart, but he has to do it while he controls the Heart suit. This takes precedence over pulling trumps.

He takes the Heart Ace and immediately plays the Diamond Jack. West wins the Ace and returns a Heart. Dummy's King wins. South leads the Diamond King, and then the Queen, on which he dumps the Heart loser.

Next, South goes after trumps. West climbs up with the Spade Ace to flash back a Heart honor but it is too late. Declarer trumps in his hand. Then South extracts trumps, takes the Club Ace, gives up a Club, and ruffs a Club in dummy. This makes ten tricks.

If declarer had pulled trumps immediately he would have gone down. West would win the Ace and play another Heart. Then, when declarer knocked out the Diamond Ace, West would seize the Heart 10. The opponents still would be due a Club trick. Down one.

To Save an Entry to Dummy. When dummy has a long side suit and is short of entries, it is sometimes imperative to draw trumps piecemeal, delaying complete extraction until dummy's long suit is established. We'll go into this in Chapter III when we study Suit Development.

To Save a "Busy" Trump. Avoid pulling a trump that's "busy" protecting you against a suit held by an opponent. Keep the busy trump aboard until you establish your side tricks and are ready to sail.

It's a fascinating strategy and here's an example:

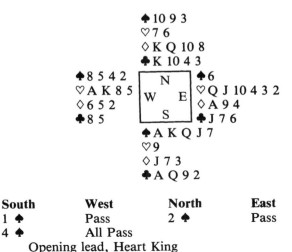

```
                    ♠ 10 9 3
                    ♡ 7 6
                    ◇ K Q 10 8
                    ♣ K 10 4 3
      ♠ 8 5 4 2        N        ♠ 6
      ♡ A K 8 5    W      E     ♡ Q J 10 4 3 2
      ◇ 6 5 2                    ◇ A 9 4
      ♣ 8 5          S          ♣ J 7 6
                    ♠ A K Q J 7
                    ♡ 9
                    ◇ J 7 3
                    ♣ A Q 9 2
```

South	West	North	East
1 ♠	Pass	2 ♠	Pass
4 ♠	All Pass		

Opening lead, Heart King

West starts off with the King of Hearts, then the Ace. Declarer ruffs the second Heart. His accounting shows only one more loser, the Diamond Ace, so he's headed for an overtrick. He starts after trumps and gets stung on the second round. East fails to follow. West started with four Spades!

There is danger ahead, and if declarer doesn't watch his step he's going to lose control of the hand and go down. He has to stop leading trumps until he knocks out the Diamond Ace. Whoever has it will lead back a Heart. He can't afford to ruff again in his hand because he needs every trump he has to pull West's. He must have a trump in dummy to stand guard over Hearts.

Is this delay in drawing trumps a threat to the contract? No. If the Diamonds are unevenly divided and West gets to ruff a Diamond, declarer still gets ten tricks.

Thus a careful declarer can make 5 Spades. A careless declarer who pulls all the adversary's trumps goes down a trick. He takes five Spade tricks and four Clubs, but when East wins the Diamond Ace, East merrily runs Hearts and gets all the rest.

Preserving the trump that's "busy" keeping the Hearts at bay rescues the contract.

These hands illustrate over and over again why an ambitious bridge player lays a plan no matter how easy a hand appears to be. Failing to lead trumps immediately may cost the contract; leading trumps with blind devotion may be equally perilous. It pays to plan the play.

Trump Management Drill

(1) (a) North opens the Heart King against 5 Clubs by West. How would you plan West's play?

```
♠ A 5 4        ┌─────┐    ♠ 7 3
♡ 6 3          │  N  │    ♡ A 8 7
◊ K Q 5        │W   E│    ◊ A J 9 7 4
♣ K Q 10 4 2   │  S  │    ♣ J 5 3
               └─────┘
```

(b) Suppose you were East in 5 Diamonds and South led the Spade King, what would your plans be?

(2) North opens a trump against West's 4 Spades. As West, how would you plan the campaign? What are the first three tricks?

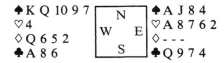

```
♠ K Q 10 9 7   ┌─────┐    ♠ A J 8 4
♡ 4            │  N  │    ♡ A 8 7 6 2
◊ Q 6 5 2      │W   E│    ◊ - - -
♣ A 8 6        │  S  │    ♣ Q 9 7 4
               └─────┘
```

(3) North opens the Heart Queen. As West, how do you propose to make 4 Spades?

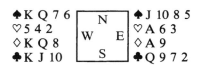

```
♠ K Q 7 6      ┌─────┐    ♠ J 10 8 5
♡ 5 4 2        │  N  │    ♡ A 6 3
◊ K Q 8        │W   E│    ◊ A 9
♣ K J 10       │  S  │    ♣ Q 9 7 2
               └─────┘
```

(4) Against West's 4 Hearts, North leads the Club Jack. South wins the Ace and leads a trump. As declarer, where do you win the trump and how do you proceed?

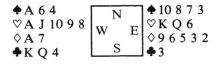

```
♠ A 6 4        ┌─────┐    ♠ 10 8 7 3
♡ A J 10 9 8   │  N  │    ♡ K Q 6
◊ A 7          │W   E│    ◊ 9 6 5 3 2
♣ K Q 4        │  S  │    ♣ 3
               └─────┘
```

5. Don't Underestimate an Opponent

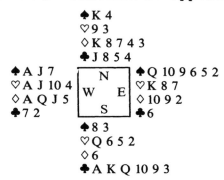

North deals
East-West vulnerable

North	East	South	West
Pass	Pass	1 ♣	Double
2 ♣	2 ♠	3 ♣	4 ♠

Opening lead, Diamond 6

This hand arose at the 1980 Nationals in the finals of the Women's Life Masters' Pairs. It was played at 50 tables and almost always the contract was 4 Spades and the lead the Diamond 6.

At one table declarer, reviewing the bidding, silently wondered, "South bid Clubs, North raised Clubs, and South bid Clubs again. Why is she leading a Diamond? That card's a singleton!"

Pausing to analyze the whole picture, East found four possible losers in the master hand — the trump King, the Diamond King, a Club, and a Heart. Then she realized she could shed a Heart on one of dummy's Diamonds. That cut the losers to three. Even if both Kings were offside, the contract was airtight, *unless somebody trumped one of her winners*. Henceforth all her thoughts were devoted to trying to keep South from getting a Diamond ruff.

Refusing the Diamond finesse, East seized dummy's Ace, then — refusing another finesse — she plunked down the Spade Ace. Next, she brought out another Spade and North won the King.

North played the Diamond King. South, unable to follow suit, dropped the Club 10, an urgent signal that she was out of trumps and wanted a Club shift. North complied. South won the Club 9, tried the Club King, but declarer ruffed. East played dummy's two Diamond winners (dropping a Heart from her hand), cashed the Ace-King of Hearts, and claimed her game.

At another table East erred at trick one by risking a Diamond finesse. Her folly led to disaster. North stepped out with the Diamond King and shot back a Diamond for partner to ruff.

This South was Portia Miller of Pittsburgh, and Portia began to thirst for more. She daringly played the Club 3, underleading the Ace-King-Queen! North produced the Jack, returned another Diamond, and Portia trumped again. North still had to get the trump King, so this East went down two, vulnerable. The American Contract Bridge League's news sheet chronicled the play under the headline, "Portia Hits the Jack-pot." The 200 score was a top over all North-Souths.

At another table declarer cleared the first hurdle by immediately winning the Diamond Ace, but stumbled over the next hurdle by attempting the Spade finesse, losing to North's King. North cashed the Diamond King, on which South played the Club 3, saying, "Don't lead a Club." So North played a Diamond and South trumped. Then South won a Club. Setting the contract one trick earned this North-South pair 100.

What happened to our East heroine who refused the Diamond finesse, refused the trump finesse, and came in with her contract? She tallied 620 points (120 for tricks and, at duplicate, 500 for the game).

Bridge is simply not a game where you can play now and think later.

6. Postpone Pulling Trumps When You Have a Reason

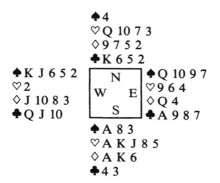

```
                    ♠ 4
                    ♡ Q 10 7 3
                    ◇ 9 7 5 2
                    ♣ K 6 5 2
   ♠ K J 6 5 2      ┌─────────┐      ♠ Q 10 9 7
   ♡ 2              │    N    │      ♡ 9 6 4
   ◇ J 10 8 3       │ W     E │      ◇ Q 4
   ♣ Q J 10         │    S    │      ♣ A 9 8 7
                    └─────────┘
                    ♠ A 8 3
                    ♡ A K J 8 5
                    ◇ A K 6
                    ♣ 4 3
```

East deals
All vulnerable

East	South	West	North
Pass	1 ♡	Pass	2 ♡
Pass	4 ♡	All Pass	

Opening lead, Club Queen

When dummy hit the table, a cautious South stopped to study and found five losing tricks in his hand — two Spades, a Diamond, and two Clubs. However, his worries quickly faded when he saw dummy could trump those little Spades and pare the losers down to three.

To get on with the play, the defenders won two Club tricks and led another round which declarer trumped. Then he started pulling the opponents' Hearts. When all the outstanding trumps failed to fall on the second round, he abandoned trumps momentarily. He had a job for those two remaining Hearts in dummy.

He played the Spade Ace, ruffed a Spade in dummy, got back to his hand with a Diamond, and ruffed another Spade with dummy's last trump. Then South crossed back to his hand with another Diamond to draw the last missing trump.

He wrapped up ten tricks following a simple bit of advice: Don't draw dummy's trumps when you need them to ruff your losers.

7. First Things First

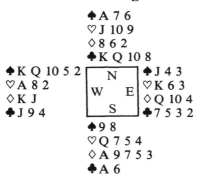

♠ A 7 6
♡ J 10 9
◇ 8 6 2
♣ K Q 10 8

♠ K Q 10 5 2
♡ A 8 2
◇ K J
♣ J 9 4

♠ J 4 3
♡ K 6 3
◇ Q 10 4
♣ 7 5 3 2

♠ 9 8
♡ Q 7 5 4
◇ A 9 7 5 3
♣ A 6

South deals
East-West vulnerable

South	West	North	East
Pass	1 ♠	Pass	2 ♠
All Pass			

Opening lead, Club King

South put his Club Ace on top of partner's King to unblock the suit and returned the Club 6. North collected two more Club tricks. Deciding he had milked Clubs dry, North switched to the Heart Jack. South signaled his pleasure with the 7, and declarer won the Ace.

Having lost three tricks, West faced three more losers — the trump Ace, the Diamond Ace, and a Heart. He foresaw a way to eliminate the Heart loser if he acted immediately.

He played the Diamond King. South won the Ace and played back a Heart. Dummy's King won. Declarer played the Diamond Queen and then the 10, dropping a losing Heart from his hand.

Then — and only then — was it safe to lead trumps. On the Spade Queen, North hopped up with the Ace and laid down the Heart 10. It was too late. Declarer had prepared for this eventuality. Having disposed of a Heart he was ready to trump the trick. School was out for the defenders. West pulled the rest of the trumps and claimed, taking the eight tricks he bargained for.

Declarer's timing was the secret to his success. He established the Diamonds while he still retained a Heart control. Suppose for a moment he first had pulled trumps. An opponent would win the Ace and return another Heart. Later when the opponents won the Diamond Ace they could cash a Heart and set the contract. That would be one in the drink.

8. It Works Like Magic

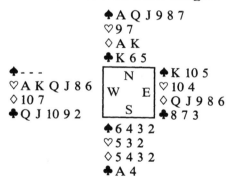

```
                ♠ A Q J 9 8 7
                ♡ 9 7
                ◊ A K
                ♣ K 6 5
  ♠ - - -              N           ♠ K 10 5
  ♡ A K Q J 8 6                    ♡ 10 4
  ◊ 10 7          W       E        ◊ Q J 9 8 6
  ♣ Q J 10 9 2        S            ♣ 8 7 3
                ♠ 6 4 3 2
                ♡ 5 3 2
                ◊ 5 4 3 2
                ♣ A 4
```

West deals
North-South vulnerable

West	North	East	South
1 ♡	Double	1 NT	Pass
4 ♡	4 ♠	All Pass	

Opening lead, Heart 10

West won two Hearts and led a third round. North ruffed with the Spade Jack. East, also void of Hearts, could have overruffed but instead discarded a Diamond.

Declarer crossed to dummy via the Club Ace and led a low Spade. When West was unable to follow, North played the Ace and East followed with the 5. Now East sat back and waited for his two trump tricks for he now held the King-10 over declarer's Q-9-8-7.

So it happened declarer lost two Spade tricks along with the two Hearts and was down one. The contract was broken on the third trick when East made a fine strategic play.

Why didn't East overruff declarer's Spade Jack? What difference did it make? Isn't a trick a trick? Not always. Imagine, for a horrible moment, East had played the trump King on top of the Jack. Declarer would have had no problem. Declarer's Ace-Queen could easily gobble up East's 10-5. When East abstained from overtrumping, East built up a second trump trick for himself, promoting his 10 into a winner.

Here's a tip on overruffing: With a natural trump winner flanked by a 10 or a 9, it is seldom advantageous to overruff an honor with an honor. However, it is wise to overruff declarer's small trump with a spot card. You do well to win a trick with a small trump.

III. THE WIZARDRY OF SUIT DEVELOPMENT

The finesse is a rock of a play, but by comparison suit establishment is a boulder. Often you can rescue a contract that appears doomed by establishing a long side suit, transforming an inconsequential little card into a winner. Knowing how to develop a suit is one of the valuable skills in bridge.

It's easy to see the power in a combination like Q-J-10-9-8 and think, "If I knock out the A-K, I can develop three tricks." It takes more foresight to look at A-5-4-3-2 and think, "If I knock out *all* the opponents' cards, I can win a trick with the 5." So next we delve into the technique of establishing a suit. As we go we'll think about the probabilities of success — sometimes there is a choice of plays and we want to choose the one with the best chance of winning.

Here's an example to entice you:

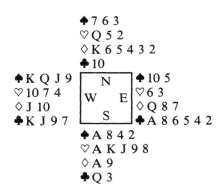

```
                  ♠ 7 6 3
                  ♡ Q 5 2
                  ♢ K 6 5 4 3 2
                  ♣ 10
   ♠ K Q J 9                    ♠ 10 5
   ♡ 10 7 4       N             ♡ 6 3
   ♢ J 10      W     E          ♢ Q 8 7
   ♣ K J 9 7      S             ♣ A 8 6 5 4 2
                  ♠ A 8 4 2
                  ♡ A K J 9 8
                  ♢ A 9
                  ♣ Q 3
```

South	West	North	East
1 ♡	Pass	2 ♡	Pass
4 ♡	All Pass		

Opening lead, Spade King

Against 4 Hearts, West tees off with the Spade King. South sees five black losers in the master hand — two Clubs and three Spades. He could cut this to four by giving up a Club right now and then ruffing a Club in dummy before pulling trumps. However, he's still confronted with four other losers, one more than he can afford.

There's one hope. If dummy's long suit can be established, South can get three pitches and make the contract. He decides to bank on Diamonds.

Accordingly, declarer wins the Spade Ace. Then, watching every trick like a hawk, he leads the Heart Ace and the Heart King. Everyone follows, so there's still one trump outstanding. Next, he makes a key play; he abandons trumps momentarily.

Cashing the Diamond Ace, he plays over to dummy's King. All follow suit. He continues another round on which East plays the Queen, the last outstanding Diamond. This means West is out of Diamonds and might be able to ruff, so declarer trumps high with the Heart Jack.

Now a low trump to dummy's Queen accomplishes two feats at once — extracts the last outstanding trump and gets the lead in dummy to run the established Diamonds, the 6-5-4. Declarer scoops in eleven winners, those little spot cards capturing tricks just like the Aces did. The Diamond investment paid off.

Was declarer lucky to find the Diamonds 3-2? Not especially. According to the Law of Averages the odds were with him the suit would divide favorably.

There's a way to plan the development of a long suit like those Diamonds, and there's a way to analyze the chances of success.

Just Four Steps

When the expert sets out to develop a long side suit, his mind whizzes through the thought process at 100 miles an hour. Replaying his thinking at a slower pace, he takes four steps:

Step One: Add the cards in the long suit in declarer's and dummy's hands.

Step Two: Determine the number the opponents hold.

Step Three: Estimate the probable distribution of the outstanding cards.

Step Four: Check the entries needed to the hand with the long suit.

Let's walk through the previous hand taking these four steps.

Step One: Declarer and dummy hold eight Diamonds.

Step Two: The opponents hold five.

Step Three: If those five Diamonds divide three in one opponent's hand and two in the other, the suit will be established after three rounds are played.

Step Four: It will take three leads to exhaust the opponents of Diamonds, and an entry outside the suit to return to dummy's winners. The suit itself enables declarer to play three rounds — the Ace, the 9 to the King, and then come off dummy with another Diamond — so one additional entry is necessary. The sole outside entry is the trump Queen.

In establishing a side suit with a trump as the only entry, it's usually necessary to delay the extraction of trumps until the side suit is set up.

Suppose the outstanding Diamonds had been divided 4-1; the whole plan would fail. Even worse, if they were divided 5-0, declarer would have lost his Diamond Ace to a little trump and gone down two tricks. Therefore, it's wise to know something about the chances of each possible division. There is a simple formula.

The Odd-Even Rule

The Odd-Even Rule states that whenever there is an odd number of cards out against you — suppose it's five (an odd number) — they usually are evenly divided, three in one opponent's hand and two in the other's. That's as even as you can divide five cards.

Whenever there is an even number of cards outstanding — say six (an even number) — they are usually unevenly divided. Most of the time they split four in one hand and two in the other.

You can prove the rule for yourself with these statistics:

Cards Outstanding	Divide	Percentage
7	4-3	62.2
	5-2	30.5
	6-1	6.8
	7-0	.5
6	4-2	48.5
	3-3	35.5
	5-1	14.5
	6-0	1.5
5	3-2	67.8
	4-1	28.3
	5-0	3.9
4	3-1	49.7
	2-2	40.7
	4-0	9.6
3	2-1	78.0
	3-0	22.0
2	1-1	52.0
	2-0	48.0

It Takes Entries

As you have just witnessed, the problem of establishing a suit is closely linked to entries. There's no use having winners if you can't reach them. Suppose declarer had extracted all the trumps before he developed dummy's Diamonds, or if he shortsightedly trumped a Club with one of dummy's three trumps. He then would have no way to reach dummy's Diamond winners. By delaying the drawing of that last trump, he held onto the entry to the hand with the long suit.

Counting the number of necessary entries is a Jonah to some people, but there is an easy way. (There's an easy way to do almost everything in bridge if you just know how.) Ask yourself how many times a suit must be played to establish it, and then add one more to get back to it. Check carefully how many rounds of play the suit itself will furnish.

Let's try the four steps on some common holdings:

$$\Diamond \text{A K Q 2}$$

```
   N
W      E
   S
```

$$\Diamond \text{5 4}$$

Step One: You have six Diamonds.

Step Two: The opponents have seven. Since one opponent is sure to have four cards, there is no way to establish dummy's fourth Diamond. The suit just isn't long enough. Don't waste any more time trying to create a trick there.

$$\Diamond \text{A K 4 3 2}$$

```
   N
W      E
   S
```

$$\Diamond \text{5}$$

Step One: Again you hold six Diamonds, but here dummy's suit is longer so you have a chance.

Step Two: The opponents have seven cards in the suit.

Step Three: The Odd-Even Rule says seven cards usually divide 4-3, so you're a favorite to establish one little card.

Step Four: How many entries will it take? The suit has to be played five times — four times to pull the opponents' Diamonds and then once more to collect the winner. The suit itself will furnish three rounds — declarer's 5 to the Ace, cash the King, and come off dummy for the third round. You need to reach dummy two more times, once to knock out the last outstanding Diamond and once more to cash the established winner. Check the other suits to see if they contain two entries; if they don't, forget it.

◊ A 5 4 3 2

◊ 7 6

On this one you walk faster. You have seven cards in the suit, the opponents six. The Odd-Even Rule says those six are most likely to split 4-2 (45.5%). You might get lucky and find them 3-3 (35.5%). Notice that if you can withstand the 4-2 break, you have an 81% bet to establish a trick!

Counting on the 4-2 split, you're going to have to run the suit four times to pick up the opponents' Diamonds; then you need one entry to cross back. If you play with care the suit itself will furnish three rounds — play the 6 and give away a round, then the 7 to the Ace, and come off dummy with a third round. Thus, you require two entries outside the suit.

◊ A 5 4 3 2

◊ K 7 6

Here you break into a trot. You have eight cards; the opponents have five, which most often split 3-2. This means the suit probably will be established in three rounds. The suit itself will furnish all three entries — lead the King, then the 6 and surrender a round, and then the 7 to dummy's Ace. Now you're in dummy ready to run the winners.

Some players hate to lose a trick, so they postpone the pain as long as possible. When you have to give the opponents a trick, as you obviously do in this situation, give it to them early and hold onto a stopper. If the suit happens to break badly you are still in control.

You Hold 5-2; They Hold 6

Now we meet a hand with a long suit with an even number of cards outstanding. To test your mettle you have to make a choice between developing a suit or trying another line of play. The key is in the planning.

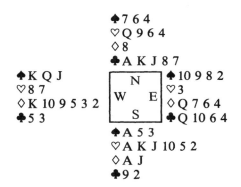

South	West	North	East
1 ♡	Pass	3 ♡	Pass
3 ♠	Pass	4 ♣	Pass
6 ♡	All Pass		

Opening lead, Spade King

After North responded with a jump raise, South became slam-minded and started cue-bidding Aces. When North showed the Club Ace, South jumped to 6 Hearts.

When dummy came down South's enthusiasm began to dwindle because he found two losing Spades. (There was a Diamond loser, too, but that didn't worry him because dummy could trump it.)

It didn't make any sense to duck the opening lead, so declarer won the Spade Ace and pulled trumps in two rounds. Now what?

Thought 1: He could take the Club finesse. If the Jack won he could drop a Spade loser on the extra Club winner.

Thought 2: He could decline the finesse and try to establish a small Club. He has seven Clubs, so the opponents have six. The Odd-Even Rule says they're probably dealt 4-2. If he plays four rounds, the opponents should be out of Clubs and he'd have a winner on which he could dump a Spade.

That necessitates leading Clubs four times and then getting back again to cash the winner. The suit itself will provide three rounds — the Ace, the King, and a third round ruffed — and the trump suit offers the other two entries.

The finesse has a 50% chance of winning since the Queen would be dealt to West half the time and to East half the time. Establishing a little Club has an overwhelming chance because it works if the opposing Clubs are 4-2 or 3-3, 84%. A wise declarer goes with the odds and, as you see, can establish Clubs and make his slam.

In the long run, those extra chances are the difference between being lucky and unlucky.

You Hold 6-1; They Hold 6

Whenever you hold seven cards in a suit, with six in one hand and one in the other, there is an excellent chance of two extra tricks with the fifth and sixth cards, providing, of course, you can get across the Rubicon to your winners.

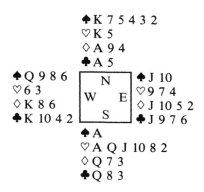

South	West	North	East
1 ♡	Pass	1 ♠	Pass
3 ♡	Pass	4 NT	Pass
5 ♡	Pass	6 ♡	All Pass

Opening lead, Heart 6

Fearing the lead from one of his honors would give declarer a soft trick, West makes the safe opening of the Heart 6.

Declarer's inventory discloses four losers in the master hand, two Diamonds and two Clubs. He could throw one loser on the Spade King, but he is still two short. Where can he unearth two tricks?

The richest source is Spades. Since he holds seven, the opponents hold six — an even number — so they're probably 4-2. If he can lead Spades four times, he might establish two winners and make the slam.

Counting entries here requires loving care. Notice one entry will account for two rounds because he can play the King, win it, and still be in dummy to continue another. The first round would be the Ace. Then, Entry One to reach the King and play another Spade, trumping; Entry Two to run the fourth round, and Entry Three to reap the winners. The two Aces and the trump King will do very nicely.

Accordingly, South takes the opening trump in the closed hand and plays the Spade Ace to unblock the suit. He then leads a trump to the board's King. Everyone follows, so there is one more trump out and declarer makes a mental note to draw it the next time he's in his hand.

He plays a small Spade from dummy, trumping with a high Heart, and then pauses to pull that stray trump. Now, back to establishing Spades. He plays over to the Diamond Ace, cashes dummy's Spade King, discarding a Diamond from his hand, and leads a fourth round of Spades, trumping. Crossing back via the Club Ace, declarer brings forth the Spade 7 and the 5, which are his slam-going tricks and allow him to pitch a Diamond loser and a Club loser.

Notice he carefully delayed cashing the Spade King until the last trump was extracted. If he happened to find an unfortunate Spade split, he didn't want that King guillotined.

You Hold 5-1; They Hold 7

Here's an illustration from a recent tournament to show what you can expect to happen when you have a side suit divided 5-1:

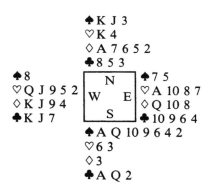

```
              ♠ K J 3
              ♡ K 4
              ◇ A 7 6 5 2
              ♣ 8 5 3
♠ 8                          ♠ 7 5
♡ Q J 9 5 2    N            ♡ A 10 8 7
◇ K J 9 4    W   E          ◇ Q 10 8
♣ K J 7        S            ♣ 10 9 6 4
              ♠ A Q 10 9 6 4 2
              ♡ 6 3
              ◇ 3
              ♣ A Q 2
```

South	West	North	East
1 ♠	Pass	2 ◇	Pass
3 ♠	Pass	4 ♠	All Pass

Opening lead, Heart Queen

On the first trick declarer rose with the Heart King. East won the Ace, cashed the 10, then switched to the Club 10. Declarer finessed the Queen, West hopped up with the King and shot back the Club Jack. Declarer won the Ace.

If you were South, what would you do next? You've lost three tricks and still hold a Club loser.

Do you see the latent power in dummy's Diamonds? Your analysis might go this way. You have six Diamonds, the opponents seven. By the Odd-Even Rule seven usually divide 4-3, so you probably can establish dummy's fifth Diamond.

Checking entries, you have to run Diamonds five times, four to strip the opponents and a fifth time to collect the established card. That requires five entries. The suit itself will let you run two rounds; you have two entries in the King-Jack of trumps. If you're smart enough to hold onto the Spade deuce, you can inch your way to dummy again with the Spade 3. Good plan. Proceed.

You play a Diamond to the Ace and return a Diamond, ruffing with the trump Ace; the trump 9 to the Jack puts you on the board to lead another Diamond, ruffed with the Spade Queen. The trump 10 to dummy's King permits you to lead the fourth round of Diamonds, trumped high, as the last outstanding Diamond falls.

The deuce of Spades to the trey gets you into dummy to play the glorious Diamond 7, your game-going trick. The little card had its day. So did good planning.

You Hold 5-2; They Hold 6

Lots of people would go down in this slam and then complain about their bad luck. You might want to cover up the East-West cards and plan the campaign by yourself. If so, go ahead and have some fun.

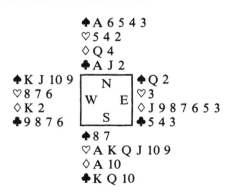

All vulnerable

South	West	North	East
1 ♡	Pass	1 ♠	Pass
4 ♡	Pass	5 ♡	Pass
6 ♡	All Pass		

Opening lead, Club 9

Starting with two losers in the master hand — a Spade and a Diamond — you cast about for a way to get rid of one. The only possibility you find is the Spade suit. You hold seven so the opponents hold six, which probably will split 4-2. You'll have to lead Spades five times, four to take all theirs and once to collect your winner. The suit itself will allow you to run three rounds if you duck the first round. Next time, lead to the Ace and return a Spade, ruffing. So you need two entries to dummy outside the suit. It's your lucky day. The Clubs will do it if you win the opening lead with the King or Queen, holding onto the 10 to reach dummy with the Jack. (See what a good guy you are, planning the whole hand before playing to the first trick.)

Accordingly, you win trick one with the Club King. You extract the outstanding trumps in three rounds. Leading a little Spade, you duck in dummy. East wins and returns a Diamond. Don't waiver! Stick to your battle plan. Pop up with the Ace!

You play a Spade to dummy's Ace and come off dummy with another Spade, ruffing. Now the Club 10 to the Jack gets you back on the board to lead the Spade 5. You trump. Finally, the Club Ace is your entry to the board to reach the established Spade 6 which brings home the little slam.

Since you were vulnerable, that little slam was worth 1,630 on the scorepad — 750 for the vulnerable slam, 700 for the rubber, and 180 for the trick score.

Principles Apply in No Trump

In almost every No Trump hand you establish a long suit. The difference between No Trump and suit contracts is, of course, that in No Trump you can't ruff out losers. You just concede them. Since the opponents' natural instinct is to try to set you, every time you duck a round they get a chance to try to do you in. Make sure you work on the holding that promises the best result. The maneuvers you've learned for suit establishment make you a more resourceful No Trump declarer.

The Strong 5-2 or the Weaker 5-3?

The anatomy of this hand epitomizes the story of suit establishment:

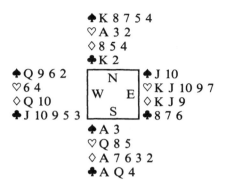

```
                    ♠ K 8 7 5 4
                    ♡ A 3 2
                    ◇ 8 5 4
                    ♣ K 2
    ♠ Q 9 6 2         ┌─────┐      ♠ J 10
    ♡ 6 4             │  N  │      ♡ K J 10 9 7
    ◇ Q 10          W │     │ E    ◇ K J 9
    ♣ J 10 9 5 3      │  S  │      ♣ 8 7 6
                      └─────┘
                    ♠ A 3
                    ♡ Q 8 5
                    ◇ A 7 6 3 2
                    ♣ A Q 4
```

South	West	North	East
1 NT	Pass	3 ♠	Pass
3 NT	All Pass		

Opening lead, Club Jack

You have seven ready-made tricks and have to find two more. You have two long suits. The Spades are stronger; the Diamonds are longer. Without looking at the East-West hands, see if you can choose the lucky way to play the hand.

Your analysis, please!

In Spades you have seven cards, so the opponents hold six. By the Odd-Even Rule those six split 4-2 more often than they split 3-3, so most of the time you can net only one extra trick.

Diamonds? The spots are so small many declarers would fail to examine the suit. You have eight, the opponents five, an uneven number. Theirs probably will divide evenly — 3-2. By surrendering two tricks, the chances are you will get two back. It's enough to bring in your contract. You decide to go with the longer suit.

In keeping with the principle of conserving entries to the hand with the long suit, you win trick one with dummy's Club King and play a low Diamond, ducking. West wins and returns the Club 10. You win in your hand and again lead a little Diamond, surrendering another trick. West wins, plays another Club, and you're in with the Ace. Your Diamond Ace rounds up the last outstanding Diamond and your Diamond 7 and 6 bring in the contract.

Synopsis

When you need to establish a side suit and you have a choice of two suits, prefer the suit where the opponents hold an odd number of cards (like the Diamonds) rather than a suit where they hold an even number of cards (like the Spades).

Suit Establishment Drill

(1) Against West's 3 No Trump, North leads the Diamond Jack.

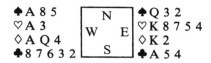

♠ A 8 5   ♠ Q 3 2
♡ A 3   ♡ K 8 7 5 4
◇ A Q 4   ◇ K 2
♣ 8 7 6 3 2   ♣ A 5 4

How many tricks does West need to create? Select the best place to look. Why?

(2) Against West's 6 Clubs, North leads the Heart Queen.

♠ A K   ♠ Q 4
♡ A K 4   ♡ 7 5 2
◇ 6 3   ◇ A 7 5 4 2
♣ A K J 10 9 4 ♣ Q 8 2

How would you play the hand?

(3) Against West's 6 No Trump, North leads the Diamond Jack. Declarer has only 10 winners.

♠ A K J   ♠ 9 2
♡ Q 7 5   ♡ A K J
◇ A K 8 7   ◇ Q 5 2
♣ 9 7 4   ♣ A K 6 5 3

In which suits are there potential winners? What is the best line of play?

(4) Against 4 Spades, North leads the Club Queen. The opponents quickly snatch three tricks, then switch to a Heart.

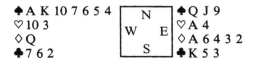

♠ A K 10 7 6 5 4 ♠ Q J 9
♡ 10 3   ♡ A 4
◇ Q   ◇ A 6 4 3 2
♣ 7 6 2   ♣ K 5 3

Declarer wins the Ace but still faces a Heart loser. What can he do?

9. Looking Down the Road

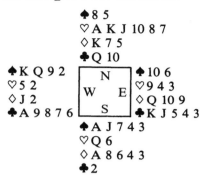

```
              ♠8 5
              ♡A K J 10 8 7
              ◇K 7 5
              ♣Q 10
   ♠K Q 9 2       N        ♠10 6
   ♡5 2                    ♡9 4 3
   ◇J 2       W     E      ◇Q 10 9
   ♣A 9 8 7 6     S        ♣K J 5 4 3
              ♠A J 7 4 3
              ♡Q 6
              ◇A 8 6 4 3
              ♣2
```

North deals
North-South vulnerable

North	East	South	West
1 ♡	Pass	1 ♠	Pass
2 ♡	Pass	3 ◇	Pass
3 ♡	Pass	4 ♡	All Pass

Opening lead, Heart 3

East read the bidding like an open book. When South bid Spades and Diamonds, then raised Hearts, he sounded short in Clubs. Convinced declarer would want to ruff Clubs in dummy, East kicked off with a trump. His strategy was to cut down dummy's ruffing power.

North checked off four losers in the master hand. With any other lead he could have trumped a Club in dummy and easily made his game. He simply could have given away one Club, then the enemy could remove one of dummy's Hearts, but there would still be one left for a ruff and bingo! He'd have ten tricks.

Now declarer had to search for a place to put one of those losers. No use leading a Club now trying still to get a ruff. Whoever won, East or West, would see through his scheme and shoot back another Heart to snatch away dummy's sole remaining trump. He had to find another way to manufacture a trick.

Could he establish a Spade or a Diamond? The Diamonds were longer and stronger, so it was more sensible to try them. He had eight and the opponents had five. If those five broke 3-2, he could create two winners. The odds were heavily in favor of this distribution existing.

Wait! Are there enough entries to dummy? The Diamond suit itself would allow declarer to run three rounds, and the Spade Ace was another entry. The mission appeared highly promising.

Back to the play, declarer won the first trick with the Heart Ace and pulled trumps in three rounds. Then he took the Diamond King and played the Diamond 7, ducking. West's Jack won. West cashed the Club Ace and played another Club to partner's King. The opponents now had three tricks.

East played the Spade 10 and dummy's Ace won. The Diamond Ace brought in the last outstanding Diamond and another Diamond provided a parking place for declarer's losing Spade. Now all his cards were high and he claimed. If the opponents hadn't been so quick to grab their Clubs he would have made an overtrick.

10. One Shot is Better Than None

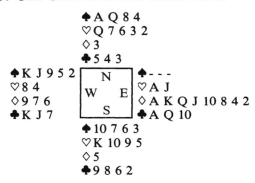

```
                    ♠ A Q 8 4
                    ♡ Q 7 6 3 2
                    ◊ 3
                    ♣ 5 4 3
   ♠ K J 9 5 2      ┌─────────┐      ♠ - - -
   ♡ 8 4            │    N    │      ♡ A J
   ◊ 9 7 6          │  W   E  │      ◊ A K Q J 10 8 4 2
   ♣ K J 7          │    S    │      ♣ A Q 10
                    └─────────┘
                    ♠ 10 7 6 3
                    ♡ K 10 9 5
                    ◊ 5
                    ♣ 9 8 6 2
```

East deals
East-West vulnerable

East	South	West	North
2 ◊	Pass	2 ♠	Pass
3 ◊	Pass	4 ◊	Pass
7 ◊	All Pass		

Opening lead, Diamond 5

Surveying dummy, declarer saw a feast of winners, but a slower analysis disclosed he was one trick shy. He had a losing Heart. Was there any possible place to put it?

The only hope was to establish a Spade. He had five, the opponents eight. If they happened to break 4-4 he could set up dummy's fifth Spade. Or, if they were distributed in any other manner, the King would become a winner anytime the Ace was in the hand with the short Spades. Declarer had to try it because it was the only chance he had.

Developing Spades would require four, maybe even five entries to the dummy. There were three in the trump suit; the King-Jack of Clubs made two more. It would require careful unblocking to preserve them.

Winning the first trick with dummy's Diamond 6, declarer was careful to put under it the Diamond 2 from his own hand. He led a Spade. North jumped up with the

Queen but declarer trumped with a high Diamond. Next, the Diamond 4 to dummy's 7 got him back on the board to lead a second Spade. Again he used a big Diamond to ruff.

Next the Club Queen was overtaken by dummy's King to lead a third round of Spades and trump. Then he played the Club 10 to the Jack. Now he led a fourth round of Spades. On this trick the Ace of Spades came tumbling down. Declarer ruffed it high gleefully.

The carefully preserved 8 of trumps was the ticket that got declarer to dummy via the Diamond 9. Then he brought forth the Spade King to bring in the grand slam.

Keeping on the lookout for entries is a very important part of declarer play. East needed every one he had to make his grand slam and he started nursing them at trick one.

11. Giving to Get

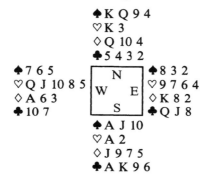

```
                    ♠ K Q 9 4
                    ♡ K 3
                    ◇ Q 10 4
                    ♣ 5 4 3 2
    ♠ 7 6 5                        ♠ 8 3 2
    ♡ Q J 10 8 5     N             ♡ 9 7 6 4
    ◇ A 6 3        W   E           ◇ K 8 2
    ♣ 10 7           S             ♣ Q J 8
                    ♠ A J 10
                    ♡ A 2
                    ◇ J 9 7 5
                    ♣ A K 9 6
```

South deals
All vulnerable

South	West	North	East
1 NT	Pass	2 ♣	Pass
2 ◇	Pass	3 NT	

Opening lead, Heart Queen

As declarer at 3 No Trump, you have eight golden tricks and need just one more. There are possibilities in Diamonds and Clubs. Which should you try?

Using the Queen-10 of Diamonds you can force out the Ace-King and absolutely establish your Jack-9. However, while you're doing this, the hungry opponents will regain the lead twice and you're down. Somebody at the table has five Hearts and can grab three Hearts tricks — along with two Diamonds — to set you before you can get your winners. No, you don't have time to set up Diamonds.

In Clubs you hold eight cards, the opponents five. If those five split 3-2 you can create a trick in Clubs. By giving up just one Club you get one back. This is a fine percentage play since the number of Clubs outstanding is an odd number.

You have time to set up Clubs. You don't have time to set up Diamonds.

With this plan you're ready to travel. You win trick one with the Heart King, collect four Spades, then lead a Club from dummy and give the opponents a Club trick. East wins and plays another Heart to your Ace. Now you cash the Ace-King of Clubs and watch carefully as all the opponents' Clubs fall. Your Club 9 brings home the bacon.

Indeed, bridge is such an easy game when you take the time to weigh one chance again another.

12. The Case of the Lowly 6

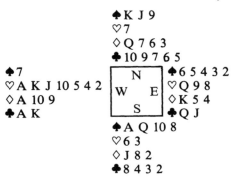

```
              ♠ K J 9
              ♡ 7
              ◇ Q 7 6 3
              ♣ 10 9 7 6 5
  ♠ 7                          ♠ 6 5 4 3 2
  ♡ A K J 10 5 4 2      N      ♡ Q 9 8
  ◇ A 10 9          W     E    ◇ K 5 4
  ♣ A K                 S      ♣ Q J
              ♠ A Q 10 8
              ♡ 6 3
              ◇ J 8 2
              ♣ 8 4 3 2
```

West deals
None vulnerable

West	North	East	South
2 ♡	Pass	3 ♡	Pass
4 NT	Pass	5 ♣	Pass
6 ♡	All Pass		

Opening lead, Club 10

Establishing a suit is a process of developing a trick that doesn't exist at the outset of a hand. Learning how to do this is a fundamental skill for an ambitious player. The opportunity to utilize it arises often.

West checked the master hand and found two losers, a Spade and a Diamond. He looked around for a way to get rid of one. Maybe he'd be lucky and the Queen-Jack of Diamonds would be a doubleton and fall, establishing his 10. He took a pessimistic attitude toward that and started studying the Spade suit.

Maybe he could develop one of dummy's Spades. Analyzing the suit, he had six so the opponents held seven, which most often split 4-3. To create a winner he'd have to play Spades five times and that would require a lot of entries. He could lead them once from his own hand, reach dummy three times in Hearts to lead them, and get over once with a Diamond. Just barely enough.

Accordingly, he won the Club Ace, led the Spade 7. North won the Spade 9 and the defenders had their book. North shot back another Club and declarer's King won.

Declarer played the trump 2 to dummy's 8, led a Spade, and trumped with the Heart Ace. Now another low Heart to dummy's 9 to lead a third round of Spades, which he ruffed with the Heart King.

All the opponents' trumps had been pulled, but he played another Heart to dummy's Queen to enable him to lead the fourth round of Spades. This brought in the last outstanding Spade as declarer ruffed.

The Diamond King provided the entry to dummy to cash the Spade 6, now the sole remaining Spade in the deck and declarer's twelfth trick. Indeed the little 6 saved the little slam.

IV. THE DANGEROUS OPPONENT

You're in a tug-of-war when you're declarer. As you struggle with all your might to reel in your contract, the opponents struggle with all their might to snatch it away from you. Usually only one foe is armed with the dangerous cards; the other is harmless. The strategy, then, is to keep the Dangerous Opponent out of the lead at all costs. There are many ways to accomplish this feat.

The first problem is to recognize which one is your Dangerous Opponent. (1) He's the player ready with an established suit to cash if he can gain the lead; or (2) he's the player in the strategic position to make a killing lead through a weakly guarded suit.

<table>
<tr><td>(1)</td><td>♡ 4 3</td><td>(2)</td><td>♣ 8 6 5</td></tr>
<tr><td>♡ K Q J 9 7</td><td>[N W E S] ♡ 8 6 5</td><td>♣ A Q 7</td><td>[N W E S] ♣ J 10 9 4</td></tr>
<tr><td></td><td>♡ A 10 2</td><td></td><td>♣ K 3 2</td></tr>
</table>

In example (1) West attacks your 3 No Trump with the Heart King and you hold back your Ace until the third round. The purpose of ducking is to interfere with subsequent communication between the East and West hands. West has two more Heart winners, but if you can maneuver to keep him out of the lead, he can never get them. *West is your Dangerous Opponent.* Any tricks you have to lose, attempt to throw to East.

In example (2) if East leads a Club, you lose three tricks. If West leads a Club, you lose only two tricks. *East is your Dangerous Opponent.* Use every artifice available to keep East from gaining the lead.

The real thrill in bridge comes when the cards are stacked against you, yet you set your wits to work and find a way to get your winners and land your contract before the opponents find a way to cash their winners and set you.

The Two-Way Finesse

The simplest maneuver to keep the Dangerous Opponent off lead is the handling of the two-way finesse. Suppose you're missing a Queen and can finesse through either opponent. Naturally you take the finesse in such a way that, if it fails, you lose to the harmless opponent. Here's an example:

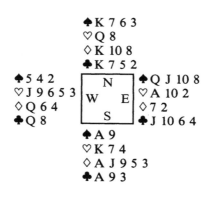

```
                ♠ K 7 6 3
                ♡ Q 8
                ◇ K 10 8
                ♣ K 7 5 2
  ♠ 5 4 2          N        ♠ Q J 10 8
  ♡ J 9 6 5 3   W     E     ♡ A 10 2
  ◇ Q 6 4          S        ◇ 7 2
  ♣ Q 8                     ♣ J 10 6 4
                ♠ A 9
                ♡ K 7 4
                ◇ A J 9 5 3
                ♣ A 9 3
```

South	West	North	East
1 NT	Pass	2 ♣	Pass
2 ◇	Pass	3 NT	All Pass

Opening lead, ♡ 5

At trick one you try dummy's Heart Queen. East pounces on it with the Ace and shoots back the 10. You duck and win the third round with the King.

Enter the villain!

West has two more good Hearts and if he regains the lead, he can set you. *West is your Dangerous Opponent.*

You have seven top tricks: two Clubs, two Diamonds, two Spades, and the Heart you've already taken. You must develop two more. Obviously, the place to find them is in Diamonds. You can finesse for the missing Queen in either direction, but there is only one correct way when you have a Dangerous Opponent.

Since West must be kept out of the lead, you finesse through West so that if you lose, you lose to East.

Accordingly you lead the Diamond 9, West follows low, dummy ducks, and, as the cards lie, the 9 wins. You continue a low Diamond, insert dummy's 10, winning again. You cash the King and the Queen falls. You cross to your hand and take the other Diamonds and wind up with 10 tricks.

When the finesse works, you get an overtrick but that is of no consequence. What is important is that by taking the finesse in that direction you guarantee the contract whether it wins or it loses. Switch the Diamond Queen to the East hand and the finesse loses, but East is bucking a brick wall. No matter what he plays, he is unable to get to his partner. You have nine tricks and your game.

It takes a clever declarer to recognize which is the Dangerous Opponent. Try this double-first cousin to that hand:

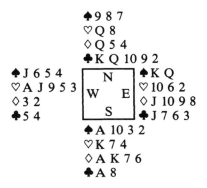

```
                    ♠9 8 7
                    ♡Q 8
                    ◇Q 5 4
                    ♣K Q 10 9 2
    ♠J 6 5 4      ┌─────────┐    ♠K Q
    ♡A J 9 5 3    │   N     │    ♡10 6 2
    ◇3 2          │ W     E │    ◇J 10 9 8
    ♣5 4          │   S     │    ♣J 7 6 3
                  └─────────┘
                    ♠A 10 3 2
                    ♡K 7 4
                    ◇A K 7 6
                    ♣A 8
```

South	West	North	East
1 NT	Pass	3 NT	All Pass

Opening lead, ♡5

Again you get a Heart lead and put up dummy's Queen. This time the Queen wins.

Enter the villain!

Who is your Dangerous Opponent? The Heart picture now is:

♡ 8

♡ A J 9 3 | N | ♡ 10 6
           | W E |
           | S |

♡ K 7

If East gains the lead and plays a Heart through your K-7, West can run the rest of the suit and down you go. If West gains the lead and continues Hearts from his side, you have another stopper and another trick.

East is your Dangerous Opponent. West is harmless.

Counting tricks you find eight: a Spade, three Diamonds, three Clubs, and the Heart you just took. You need one more. Obviously, you expect to develop Clubs.

What is the Club story? You have seven, the opponents six. Since you've studied suit establishment you expect the six outstanding Clubs to split 4-2 and the Jack more likely to be in the hand with four cards. If West has J-x-x-x, you have nothing to fear. If East has J-x-x-x, you could go down.

Being a careful declarer who conscientiously analyzes these things at the outset, at trick two you lead dummy's Club deuce and finesse the 8, which wins. You cash the Ace, get back to the board with the Diamond Queen, and run the Clubs. You turn 10 tricks.

If the Club finesse had failed and West had won that trick, he could not stop the contract whatever he returned. He could cash his Heart Ace, but then you take 10 tricks. If he doesn't cash it, you get nine.

The deep finesse was taken not caring whether it won or lost but in an attempt to establish an extra Club, in the meantime keeping the Dangerous Opponent from gaining the lead.

Choose Between Two Suits

Sometimes you have two long suits. Either would give you the contract, and each requires a finesse. Which suit do you tackle? If setting up one suit risks losing a trick to the Dangerous Opponent and setting up the other suit risks losing to the safe opponent, obviously you try the suit that loses to the safe opponent.

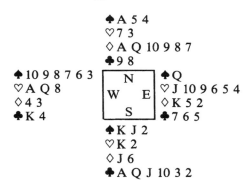

```
                    ♠ A 5 4
                    ♡ 7 3
                    ◇ A Q 10 9 8 7
                    ♣ 9 8
♠ 10 9 8 7 6 3    ┌─────────┐    ♠ Q
♡ A Q 8           │    N    │    ♡ J 10 9 6 5 4
◇ 4 3             │ W     E │    ◇ K 5 2
♣ K 4             │    S    │    ♣ 7 6 5
                  └─────────┘
                    ♠ K J 2
                    ♡ K 2
                    ◇ J 6
                    ♣ A Q J 10 3 2
```

South	West	North	East
1 ♣	Pass	1 ◇	Pass
2 ♣	Pass	3 ◇	Pass
3 NT	All Pass		

Opening lead, ♠ 10

You naturally let the opening lead ride around to your hand, East perforce playing the Queen, and you win the King. You now have three Spade tricks and two minor suit Aces and need four more tricks. Should you try to set up dummy's Diamonds or your Clubs? It makes a difference!

In both suits you have to finesse against the King, and you know how finesses are. Half of them fail. What happens if you play Diamonds and the finesse goes sour? What happens if you start on Clubs and the finesse loses?

Enter the villain!

You have a weak link in your armor — your Heart holding. If you try to develop Diamonds and East gains the lead, he can run a Heart through your K-2. If West holds the Ace, you're dead. *East is your Dangerous Opponent.* If you try to develop Clubs and the finesse fails, it loses to West who's harmless. If he leads Hearts, you have a stopper. Consequently you choose Clubs.

Crossing to dummy with the Spade Ace, you lead the Club 9 and finesse. It loses, but your game is now unbeatable. If West plays back another Spade, you win the Jack, cash five Club winners, lead a Diamond and hop up with the Ace for your ninth trick.

Suppose for a horrible moment you took the tempting Diamond finesse at trick two. After all, you were in the South hand and in position to start that suit. The finesse fails. East switches to the Heart Jack. Disaster strikes. They rattle off six tricks.

Need Two Suits; Which Comes First?

Here's a puzzle where you have two suits and have to develop both of them to bring home the game. Does it matter which suit you work on first? If you have a Dangerous Opponent, it matters a lot! See here:

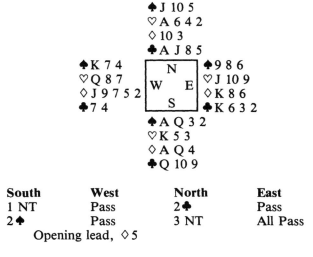

♠ J 10 5
♡ A 6 4 2
◇ 10 3
♣ A J 8 5

♠ K 7 4   ♠ 9 8 6
♡ Q 8 7   ♡ J 10 9
◇ J 9 7 5 2   ◇ K 8 6
♣ 7 4   ♣ K 6 3 2

♠ A Q 3 2
♡ K 5 3
◇ A Q 4
♣ Q 10 9

South	West	North	East
1 NT	Pass	2♣	Pass
2♠	Pass	3 NT	All Pass

Opening lead, ◇ 5

When East plays the Diamond King on trick one, you duck. You have to lose a Diamond trick sometime, and it might as well be now. You win the second round. Your study turns up only six quick winners — two Diamonds, two Hearts, one Club, and one Spade. You need three more and they're available in the black suits. Should you tackle Clubs or Spades first?

Enter the villain!

Thinking the hand through, if you play Clubs first and the finesse wins, you bring in the three tricks you need in one swoop. If it fails, East wins and returns a Diamond, dislodging your last stopper. You still need a Spade trick. When you try to knock out the Spade King, if West has it he can run his established Diamonds and it's curtains for you.

When you have only one stopper left in the threat suit — yet you might have to relinquish the lead twice — lose first to the Dangerous Opponent. There's always the likelihood the safe opponent, in the meantime, will run out of cards in the threat suit, so when he gets his trick he won't have one to lead.

West is the Dangerous Opponent. He must be disarmed first while you still have a Diamond stop. If he has an entry, it's in Spades. If he has the Club King, it's finessable. This is the reason for leading Spades before Clubs.

The play goes this way. To reach dummy you lead a Heart to the Ace, then play the Spade Jack. West probably ducks a round but on the next round wins the King and plays another Diamond. You win the Diamond Ace and collect your Spade winners.

Now you're ready for Clubs. You lead the Queen, finesse, and lose to East's King — but East hasn't a Diamond left to reach West, the deadly one. You win anything he returns and take 10 tricks — three Spades, two Hearts, two Diamonds, and three Clubs.

Step back and try the black suits in the reverse order, Clubs first. You lose a Club, three Diamonds, and a Spade, and your game dries up.

The Ducking Ploy

In establishing a long suit it is sometimes necessary for you to surrender a round. Be careful to lose it to your safe opponent. Here's an illustration:

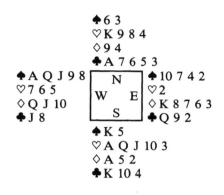

South	West	North	East
1♡	1♠	2♡	2♠
4♡	All Pass		

Opening lead, ◇ Q

Your first glimpse of dummy reveals five losers — two Spades, two Diamonds, and a Club. One Diamond can be ruffed in dummy, and if you develop Clubs in time, you can get rid of a losing Spade or two.

Enter the villain!

If East gains the lead and pokes a Spade through your K-5, you'll go down. *East is your Dangerous Opponent.* Use every means available to keep East out of the lead.

West's opening lead of the Diamond Queen indicates that East has the King of Diamonds, so you begin battle by ducking and letting harmless West win. West sends out another Diamond and you take the Ace. Pulling trumps in three rounds, you wind up in dummy.

You come off dummy with a low Club. When East follows low, you finesse the 10. You have no expectation of winning it and you don't. West takes the Jack. (If Clubs are split 3-2 the suit is established.)

West sees the jig is up (clever fellow), so he cashes the Spade Ace. You win the next Spade and have 10 tricks. If West hadn't grabbed his Spade Ace, he never would have gotten it. On the extra Club winners, you'd discard both your Spades and make 11 tricks.

Retrace your steps and see what happens if you win the first Diamond. When West wins the Club, he can play a Diamond to East's King. East then can send a Spade through your K-5 and you're a goner.

Another Ducking Ploy

Sometimes you need to be extremely cautious to circumvent your Dangerous Opponent. Consider the following Diamond distribution:

$$\diamond\,7\,6\,5\,4$$

$$\diamond\,J\,10\,9\quad\boxed{\begin{array}{c}N\\W\quad E\\S\end{array}}\quad\diamond\,Q\,8$$

$$\diamond\,A\,K\,3\,2$$

You are South and have two Diamond tricks but must have one more. You have a Dangerous Opponent. If you simply lay down the Ace and the King and surrender the third round willy nilly, you might be unlucky and lose to your Dangerous Opponent. You can exercise more control over your fate by leading *toward* the Ace-King, ready to take advantage of any card East plays.

The proper handling is required in the following deal:

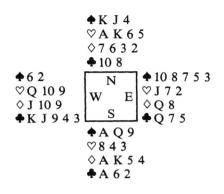

♠ K J 4	
♡ A K 6 5	
◇ 7 6 3 2	
♣ 10 8	

South	West	North	East
1 NT	Pass	2 ♣	Pass
2 ◇	Pass	3 NT	All Pass

Opening lead, ♣4

As declarer you hold back the Club Ace as long as you can, winning the third round. You clock off eight available winners — three Spades, two Hearts, two Diamonds, and the Club already before you. The best source for your ninth trick is Diamonds, but you have to give up one round to establish a long card.

Enter the villain!

West is your Dangerous Opponent. He holds the established Clubs. East is safe. You set out to exercise as much control as possible over who wins that Diamond trick.

Crossing to dummy with the Spade Jack you come off the board with a Diamond, East plays the 8, and you run up with the King. Back to the board with the Spade King, you lead another Diamond. East drops the Queen. It is ducking time! East wins the trick and is helpless. He can't get West on lead. Hopelessly he plays a Spade, you win, collect the established Diamond, take all your winners, and waltz in with nine tricks.

If you had played in a lackadaisical fashion, just plopping down the Ace-King of Diamonds, West would gain the lead, cash his Clubs, and you would end up at the bottom of the heap.

What if East had been the Dangerous Opponent? You could still control your fate with the same careful play. Leading Diamonds from dummy, when East plays the 8 you duck knowing that every Diamond out is higher than the 8. If East, instead, drops the Queen, you play high and cross back to try again.

Transfer a Loser

Here's one more weapon for your arsenal. To neutralize the Dangerous Opponent, you can sometimes transfer a loser the Dangerous Opponent could win to another suit which the harmless opponent has to win. This expert play involves some fancy footwork. It's fun.

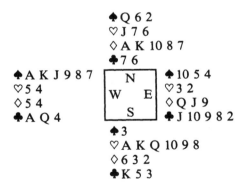

```
                    ♠ Q 6 2
                    ♡ J 7 6
                    ◇ A K 10 8 7
                    ♣ 7 6
  ♠ A K J 9 8 7    ┌─────────┐    ♠ 10 5 4
  ♡ 5 4            │    N    │    ♡ 3 2
  ◇ 5 4            │ W     E │    ◇ Q J 9
  ♣ A Q 4          │    S    │    ♣ J 10 9 8 2
                   └─────────┘
                    ♠ 3
                    ♡ A K Q 10 9 8
                    ◇ 6 3 2
                    ♣ K 5 3
```

West	North	East	South
1 ♠	Pass	Pass	2 ♡
Pass	3 ♡	Pass	4 ♡
All Pass			

Opening lead, ♠ King

Your accounting adds up five losers in the master hand — a Spade, a Diamond, and three Clubs, but you quickly observe you can throw some Club losers on dummy's long Diamonds.

Enter the villain!

There is a fly in the ointment. If East gains the lead and shoots a Club through the King, you're down. *East is the Dangerous Opponent.*

Your mission: establish Diamonds without allowing East to gain the lead. Before reading further, see if you can find a way.

On to the play. West wins the opening lead of the Spade King and shifts to the Diamond 5. Dummy's King wins. Then you make an unexpected switch. You pull out dummy's Spade Queen and, instead of trumping, discard a Diamond! West wins but is helpless. It's time to lead Clubs but he's sitting on the wrong side of the table. He plays another Diamond and dummy's Ace wins. You lead a third round of Diamonds. East plays the Queen, the master card in the suit, but you trump with the Heart Ace.

Extracting trumps in two rounds, you continue a third Heart to dummy's Jack. Then you bring out dummy's two Diamond winners and throw away two losing Clubs. This gives you 10 red tricks — six Hearts and four Diamonds.

Your startling strategy brought home the game. To recapitulate, you discarded a losing Diamond (which the Dangerous Opponent could win) on a Spade which you knew would be won by the safe opponent.

A Safety Play

Sometimes a fine declarer gives up a trick he might not have to lose in order to guarantee his contract. Here's an example of that safety play:

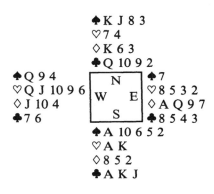

	♠ K J 8 3	
	♡ 7 4	
	◇ K 6 3	
	♣ Q 10 9 2	

South	West	North	East
1♠	Pass	2♠	Pass
4♠	All Pass		

Opening lead, ♡ Queen

When you see four possible losers, three Diamonds and a trump, you start searching for a foolproof way to land your game.

With nine cards in the trump suit, missing Q-x-x-x, the usual rule-of-thumb is to cash the Ace-King, but you don't close your eyes to the possibility of finessing. What if they happen to be 3-1 and West holds Q-x-x? He can defeat you by playing a Diamond through dummy's K-6-3. *West is your Dangerous Opponent.*

If East has Q-x-x you're secure because nothing East can lead will keep you from pointing to 10 sure tricks. *East is your safe opponent.*

Consequently, after winning the Heart King, at trick two you cash the Spade Ace, play another and finesse the Jack. You hardly care whether the Jack stands or falls. When East fails to follow, you pause to congratulate yourself for your careful forethought. Then you cash the Spade King, felling the Queen, take four Clubs, and end up with 11 tricks.

But let's say you belong to the "Eight-Ever, Nine Never" school, which woodenly plays Ace-King when holding nine cards in a suit. On this hand you'd wind up with your arm in a sling. West would win the trump Queen as early as possible, lead the Diamond Jack, and the opponents would quickly run off three Diamond tricks.

You could blame it on bad luck. It was unfortunate the Spades were 3-1 and the Queen in the wrong hand, and it was unfortunate the Diamond Ace was over the King. Nevertheless the bottom line is the safety play in Spades can cost you a trick but it can't cost you the contract.

Like most card plays, this safety play was easy. All you had to do was think of it!

Dangerous Opponent Drill

(1) Against West's 3 No Trump, North leads the Club 5.

```
♠ K 6 4          ┌─────┐          ♠ A Q 5
♡ A J 10 6       │  N  │          ♡ 5 2
◇ K 9 7        W │     │ E        ◇ A J 10 5 2
♣ A 6 4          │  S  │          ♣ 8 7 2
                 └─────┘
```

South plays the Club Jack. Assuming North has five Clubs, how would you play the hand?

(2) Against West's 3 NT, North leads the Spade 3.

```
♠ Q 7 4          ┌─────┐          ♠ K 9
♡ A Q 4 3        │  N  │          ♡ 7 2
◇ A 9          W │     │ E        ◇ K Q 10 7 5 4
♣ A Q 7 2        │  S  │          ♣ K 5 3
                 └─────┘
```

Dummy's Spade King wins the first trick. (a) Who is the Dangerous Opponent? Why? (b) Can you bring in nine tricks against any Diamond distribution?

(3) West plays 4 Spades and North opens the ♡ King.

```
♠ A K 9 7 6 5 4 2   ┌─────┐       ♠ Q J 8
♡ - - -             │  N  │       ♡ Q J
◇ K 5 2           W │     │ E     ◇ 9 7 4 3
♣ 7 6               │  S  │       ♣ A Q J 10
                    └─────┘
```

(a) Who is the Dangerous Opponent? Why? (b) Can you plan a strategy to be certain the Danger Hand never ever gains the lead?

(4) West plays 5 Diamonds and North leads the ♠ 10.

```
♠ A 8 5          ┌─────┐          ♠ Q J
♡ K 5            │  N  │          ♡ 8 6 4
◇ A 10 9 7 3   W │     │ E        ◇ K J 8
♣ A K J          │  S  │          ♣ Q 10 8 6 4
                 └─────┘
```

On trick one South rises with the Spade King and declarer wins the Ace. (a) Is there a Dangerous Opponent? (b) Can you guarantee the contract against a 4-1 trump split?

13. Going Against the Wind

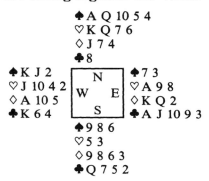

♠ A Q 10 5 4
♡ K Q 7 6
◇ J 7 4
♣ 8

♠ K J 2   ♠ 7 3
♡ J 10 4 2   ♡ A 9 8
◇ A 10 5   ◇ K Q 2
♣ K 6 4   ♣ A J 10 9 3

♠ 9 8 6
♡ 5 3
◇ 9 8 6 3
♣ Q 7 5 2

North deals
All vulnerable

North	East	South	West
1♠	2♣	Pass	2 NT
Pass	3 NT	All Pass	

Opening lead, ♠ 5

The opening lead was taken by declarer's Jack. Now he had six other instant winners, three Diamonds, two Clubs, and one Heart, for a total of seven. The best source for two more was in the Club suit where he had a two-way finesse for the missing Queen.

Finding 26 points in his hand and dummy, declarer naturally assumed the missing 14 were in the hand of the opponent who opened the bidding. If he finessed North and the finesse won, he had an overtrick.

Enter the villain!

If through some fluke South turned up with the Club Queen, South could shoot a Spade through the K-2 and wreck the contract. *South was the Dangerous Opponent.* North was harmless. Even if North won the Club finesse, the contract was secure because if North led a Spade, declarer had a stopper.

That's why declarer went against the wind, you might say, at trick two. Crossing to dummy via the Diamond

Queen, he brought out the Club Jack and finessed. It won! Next, the 10, again winning. Then a little Club to the King. Returning to dummy with the Diamond King, he collected the other Clubs, cashed two red Aces, and had ten tricks.

Meanwhile, North was squirming. All those Clubs forced him to find discards so he was down to ♠ A-Q ♡ K. Declarer gave him the Heart King, and North was end-played. He had to give West the Spade King. Thus declarer brought in eleven tricks.

There were two alternate ways declarer might have played the Clubs, both wrong.

Wrong Way I: Finesse North for the Queen, lose to South, who sends a Spade through and sinks West's ship. Declarer has a reasonable alibi, too, "On the bidding North was more likely to have the Queen."

Wrong Way II: Play a Club to the Ace, planning to finesse the next round. There's an alibi available here, too. This works if the five outstanding Clubs divide 3-2, the most common split, but fails in the actual case because the Clubs are 4-1 and require two finesses. Since you can afford to lose to the Club Queen, it makes sense to guard against all Club splits and not just consider the most likely 3-2.

14. Look Before You Leap

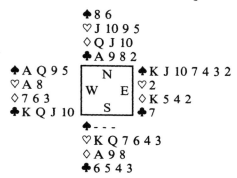

```
              ♠ 8 6
              ♡ J 10 9 5
              ◇ Q J 10
              ♣ A 9 8 2
  ♠ A Q 9 5   ┌─────────┐   ♠ K J 10 7 4 3 2
  ♡ A 8       │    N    │   ♡ 2
  ◇ 7 6 3     │ W     E │   ◇ K 5 4 2
  ♣ K Q J 10  │    S    │   ♣ 7
              └─────────┘
              ♠ - - -
              ♡ K Q 7 6 4 3
              ◇ A 9 8
              ♣ 6 5 4 3
```

East deals
None vulnerable

East	South	West	North
3 ♠	Pass	4 ♠	All Pass

Opening lead, ♡ King

East's preemptive bid gave a good description of his hand and West, with excellent trump support, quick tricks, and a respectable side suit, contracted for a game.

As custodian of the contract, it was now East's job to deliver. He checked off four possible Diamond losers and one Club loser.

With so many trumps in dummy, it was certain one Diamond loser would disappear, and the possibility of throwing other Diamonds on dummy's Clubs looked promising.

Enter the villain!

In the meantime, he didn't want North to gain the lead and push a Diamond through his King. If South held the Diamond Ace, the opponents could cash four winners before declarer got his discards.

This threat to the contract made North the Dangerous Opponent. If North could be kept out of the lead, the contract was airtight. Then, declarer devised a way. Can you find it?

At trick one he ducked in dummy, giving South a trick with the Heart King! It was a strange play, but a play with a purpose. South persisted with another Heart. As the Ace won, declarer discarded his lone Club.

The Ace and Queen of Spades brought in the trumps. The Club King was next and West jumped up with the Ace. Triumphantly, declarer trumped.

Returning to dummy with the trump 9, declarer led the three remaining Club honors and threw away three Diamond losers. Then he conceded one Diamond and claimed eleven tricks.

By surrendering a Heart trick to the safe opponent, instead of a Club to the Dangerous Opponent, declarer transferred a loser and stayed out of hot water.

What happens if South holds the Club Ace? Then declarer's safety shenanigans cost a trick, but the contract is still a certainty. On the Club King, when North follows low, declarer discards a Diamond loser and South wins the trick. Now South can take the Diamond Ace, but declarer wins the next Diamond and still scores his game.

15. First Defang the Dragon

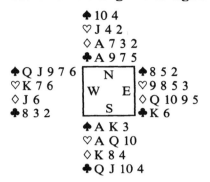

♠ 10 4
♡ J 4 2
◇ A 7 3 2
♣ A 9 7 5

♠ Q J 9 7 6
♡ K 7 6
◇ J 6
♣ 8 3 2

♠ 8 5 2
♡ 9 8 5 3
◇ Q 10 9 5
♣ K 6

♠ A K 3
♡ A Q 10
◇ K 8 4
♣ Q J 10 4

South deals
North-South vulnerable

South	West	North	East
1♣	Pass	1◇	Pass
2 NT	Pass	3 NT	All Pass

Opening lead, ♠ Queen

With only six tricks off the top, declarer began digging for three more. If the Club finesse worked, he could find all three in that suit. If it failed, he could collect only two additional tricks and would have to fall back on the Heart finesse.

If both finesses succeeded, there were 11 tricks. If the cards were perverse and both failed, it was possible to lose two Kings plus three Spades and be down one. It was a fragile position.

In danger of losing the lead twice (and with only two Spade stoppers), declarer ducked trick one and let the Spade Queen win. Next came the Spade Jack and declarer was in with the King.

Should he play Clubs or Hearts? Or did it matter?

Enter the villain!

Yes, it did matter. *West was the Dangerous Opponent;* only his long Spades could set the contract. He had to be immobilized. If he had an entry, it had to be knocked out immediately.

That's why declarer decided to attack Hearts first. Crossing to dummy via the Diamond Ace, he brought out the Heart Jack. It lost to West's King and West shelled out another Spade. Declarer won with his last Spade stopper and tried the Club finesse. It lost to East. Lo, East was out of Spades and unable to reach his partner. He tried a Diamond. Declarer won the King, took his Heart and Club winners, and squeaked in with nine tricks.

If declarer takes the Club finesse first, the whole hand dissolves. East wins and can dislodge declarer's last Spade stopper. Later when the Heart finesse fails, West can cash his Spades for down one.

16. Sighted Sub . . . Sank Same

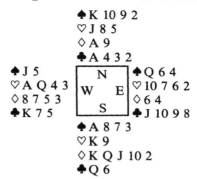

```
              ♠ K 10 9 2
              ♡ J 8 5
              ◇ A 9
              ♣ A 4 3 2
♠ J 5          ┌─────────┐      ♠ Q 6 4
♡ A Q 4 3      │    N    │      ♡ 10 7 6 2
◇ 8 7 5 3      │  W   E  │      ◇ 6 4
♣ K 7 5        │    S    │      ♣ J 10 9 8
              └─────────┘
              ♠ A 8 7 3
              ♡ K 9
              ◇ K Q J 10 2
              ♣ Q 6
```

West deals
East-West vulnerable

West	North	East	South
Pass	1♣	Pass	1◇
Pass	1♠	Pass	3♠
Pass	4♠	All Pass	

Opening lead, ♣Jack

Analyzing the lead was easy. It revealed the probable division of the Club honors. East had a sequence, probably J-10-9, but he wouldn't like to lead from the K-J-10-9, so West held the King.

Counting his liabilities, declarer came up with four possible losers, a trump, a Club, and two Hearts.

Knuckling down to some serious study, he looked for a way to eliminate one Heart loser. He could lead toward dummy's King and, if East held the Ace, all would be well. If instead West held the Ace, all would be lost.

Then he saw an alternate line of play. He could pull trumps, run the long Diamonds, and throw away all the Hearts in the closed hand. That would eliminate the Heart problem.

Enter the villain!

Meanwhile, it was imperative to keep East out of the lead so he couldn't start Hearts before declarer got his discards. *East was the Dangerous Opponent.*

So declarer covered the Club Jack with dummy's Queen (with no expectation of its winning), West tossed out the King, and declarer played the deuce!

West continued Clubs and declarer won the Ace. He led the Spade 10. When East followed low, declarer ducked in dummy. West won the Jack and was on lead once again.

With no better choice, he led a third round of Clubs. Dummy ruffed. Now came the Spade Ace and King as all the opponents' trumps rolled in.

Then declarer ran five Diamonds, throwing away all his own Hearts. This enabled him to trump a Heart for his tenth trick.

The instinctive play is to put the Ace of Clubs on top of the King, but it would be fatal in this hand. When West gets in with the Spade Jack, he can play back a Club and East is in to make the obvious switch to a Heart. Thus the opponents pilfer two Heart tricks before declarer gets to pitch his losers and the game slips away.

Once declarer ducks the first Club, he's on Easy Street. There is nothing the opponents can do against this cunning play.

V. SAFETY PLAYS

Some contracts appear to be so e-a-s-y that they slip right through your fingers. Sometimes you trust in good breaks and forget to think about the pranks in the distribution. Sometimes you get greedy for an overtrick and go down in a contract you could make. Sometimes you play too fast and see too late the clue to the case.

The first step always is to count winning or losing tricks.

When you don't have enough assets and the situation looks hopeless, *be an optimist*. Search for any possible lay of the cards that could give you the contract, take any gamble that gives you a chance. The drowning man grabs at a straw.

When the count reveals you have enough tricks, or a surplus, *be a pessimist*. Ask yourself, "What calamity can befall me?" Look around for the safest way to play the hand. Be glad to sacrifice an overtrick if that adds even a modicum of safety. Don't let 30 points above the line lure you to doom. Bring out the safety plays!

A safety play is just what the name suggests: a play made to reduce the risk of going down. Many safety plays deliberately sacrifice one trick to safeguard against losing two tricks.

There is a smorgasbord of safety plays to help you, so many it is impossible to codify them all. When you understand the principle, you can improvise them on the spot. They fall into two categories: (l) Cautious plays that are just common sense, like looking both ways before crossing a busy street. These require careful attention. (2) Scientific handling of certain combinations of face cards that are treacherous when you run into devilish distribution. These require study.

COMMON SENSE SAFETY PLAYS

1. The Duck

Of all safety plays, the duck is Number One. Here's an example from real life:

<pre>
                ♠9 6
                ♡9 5 3
                ◇A K Q 6 5 3
                ♣8 6
              ┌─────────┐
              │   N   │
              │ W   E │
              │   S   │
              └─────────┘
                ♠A Q 5 3
                ♡A K 2
                ◇4 2
                ♣A K 5 2
</pre>

South	West	North	East
1 ♣	Pass	1 ◇	Pass
2 ♠	Pass	3 ◇	Pass
3 NT	All Pass		

Opening lead, Heart 6

Surveying his prospects pleasurably, South counts eight tricks off the top and the Diamond suit is a rich source for three more. That would make eleven tricks! There's also the chance of a Spade finesse. If that should succeed, he has a dozen! The contract looks so e-a-s-y.

The optimist wins the Heart King and plays the Diamond Ace and King. Then East shows out on the second round! Now declarer takes his Diamond Queen and falls back on the Spade finesse. When that loses, he's out of steam, but he has enough breath to complain about his bad breaks.

The pessimist, looking for the most cautious approach to assure his game, tries a safety play. He leads a little Diamond from his hand and ducks in dummy, deliberately giving away a trick. This protects him against a 4-1 break and improves his chances of delivering the game. If the five outstanding Diamonds happen to split 3-2, the safety play costs him an insignificant overtrick.

This is the essence of the safety play. To improve the chances of making the required number of tricks, declarer deprives himself of a possible overtrick.

2. The Finesse: Friend and Foe

It's an automatic reflex for a bridge player to finesse for a missing King. It's the first play a beginner learns and he practices it with earnest enthusiasm. The more difficult lesson comes later when he tries to learn not to risk a finesse that endangers his contract.

Look at this example, keeping in mind that your mission is to succeed on e-a-s-y contracts:

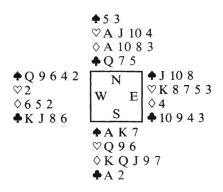

South	West	North	East
1 ◇	Pass	1 ♡	Pass
2 NT	Pass	4 ◇	Pass
4 NT	Pass	5 ♡	Pass
6 ◇	All Pass		

Opening lead, Heart 2

Declarer checks off twelve golden tricks — five Diamonds, two Spades and one Spade ruffed in dummy, one Club, and three Hearts. If West has the Heart King, it's possible to take all 13 tricks.

What card would you play from dummy? When a hand looks so e-a-s-y, step back for a moment and ask, "Is there any calamity that can befall me?"

The safety play is to climb up with the Heart Ace and pull trumps as fast as you can. After that cheerfully give away a trick to the Heart King.

When a declarer sees his slam is on ice, it's common sense to resist the finesse. The safety of the contract is the sole consideration. Nevertheless, many declarers, not thinking, not counting tricks, play low from dummy. The King comes up and another Heart is shot back for West to ruff. Now the ball game is over after the second inning.

3. Refusing a Trump Finesse

There are times to refuse a finesse even in the trump suit itself, if losing the finesse would jeopardize the contract. Here's a hand to prove the point:

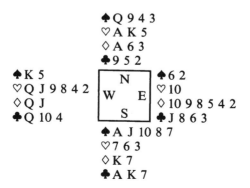

```
              ♠ Q 9 4 3
              ♡ A K 5
              ◇ A 6 3
              ♣ 9 5 2
♠ K 5          ┌─────────┐      ♠ 6 2
♡ Q J 9 8 4 2  │   N     │      ♡ 10
◇ Q J          │ W     E │      ◇ 10 9 8 5 4 2
♣ Q 10 4       │   S     │      ♣ J 8 6 3
              └─────────┘
              ♠ A J 10 8 7
              ♡ 7 6 3
              ◇ K 7
              ♣ A K 7
```

South	West	North	East
1 ♠	2 ♡	3 ♠	Pass
4 ♠	All Pass		

Opening lead, Heart Queen

Dummy's Heart King wins the first trick as East drops the Heart 10. Declarer's study shows only three losers — a trump, a Heart, and a Club. Cautiously he asks, "Is there anything that can set me?" Yes, if East ruffs dummy's Heart Ace.

Therefore, South plays the hand as carefully as possible. The Spade Queen is led from dummy. When East follows low, declarer rises with the Ace, refusing the finesse. A low trump comes next and the King wins as all the outstanding trumps fall. Now declarer's contract is as solid as the Rock of Gibraltar.

South said no to the trump finesse for a reason: West's Heart overcall was made without the Ace or King, so he must have a long suit, probably six cards. That gives East a singleton, so East can ruff the next round. Declarer can afford to lose the trump King, but he can't afford to lose a ruff to boot. That's why he took the safety play of refusing the finesse.

It's a natural instinct to finesse for a trump King, but if South had, it would have lost and West would have shot back the Heart Jack. If declarer covers with the Ace, East ruffs and later declarer must lose another Heart. If declarer plays low, East discards and ruffs the next Heart. Either way declarer goes down.

A fine declarer does not dally with unnecessary finesses when the defenders threaten to ruff. If East had held the trump King, the safety play would have cost an overtrick.

4. Neutralizing a Ruff

The following deal points out a slightly different safety play which a declarer might mishandle if he didn't stop and look ahead:

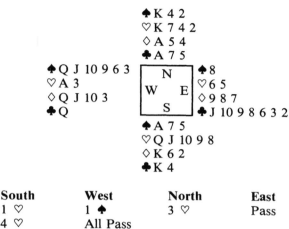

♠ K 4 2
♡ K 7 4 2
◇ A 5 4
♣ A 7 5

♠ Q J 10 9 6 3
♡ A 3
◇ Q J 10 3
♣ Q

♠ 8
♡ 6 5
◇ 9 8 7
♣ J 10 9 8 6 3 2

♠ A 7 5
♡ Q J 10 9 8
◇ K 6 2
♣ K 4

South	West	North	East
1 ♡	1 ♠	3 ♡	Pass
4 ♡	All Pass		

Opening lead, Spade Queen

Again there are only three possible losers — a trump, a Spade, and a Diamond. The hand looks so e-a-s-y it's time to ask, "Is there any abnormal distribution that can set me?" The answer is "Yes, if East, who is undoubtedly short in Spades, trumps dummy's Spade winner and two Spades are lost instead of one."

The safety play is to win the first trick with dummy's King. Then lead a trump. West is in with the Ace and plays back the Spade Jack. East can ruff, but he's ruffing on air. Declarer can play a low Spade from each hand. Now the contract is safe.

The natural instinct for declarer is to let the first trick ride to his own hand, but a cautious declarer foresees that East might ruff the second round, killing dummy's King. By letting the second Spade ride to his hand instead of the first, South is able to render the ruff harmless.

5. Common Sense Trump Plays

Many safety plays consist of handling combinations of honors to protect yourself against freakish deals. They can be worked out by counting the outstanding cards in the suit, mentally juggling those cards in different combinations, and protecting yourself against bad breaks wherever possible.

Caution: Missing J-x-x-x

The following deal illustrates a trump holding sometimes frivolously handled:

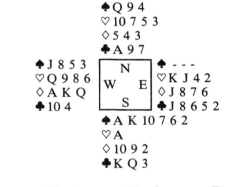

South	West	North	East
1 ♠	Pass	2 ♠	Pass
4 ♠	All Pass		

Opening lead, Diamond King

West takes the first three Diamonds and is book-in when he switches to the Club 10. South lets it ride to his Queen. The hand looks like a piece of cake, so South asks himself, "Is there any danger lurking ahead?" The answer is, "Only if the four missing trumps are all in one hand."

The solution is to first lay down one of the double honors — the King or the Ace. If either opponent holds four trumps, it is revealed on the first round and you are in a position to finesse East or West out of the Jack.

If West holds all four Spades, as in this deal, East shows out on the first round and you next finesse dummy's 9 spot. Cash the Queen, return to your hand with a Heart, and lay down the Spade Ace to extract the last trump.

If, however, East has all four trumps, you're equally safe. After cashing the King, next take the Queen and then finesse East on the way back, playing through the J-8 toward your A-10. Again you pick up the whole suit.

Look at the tragedy that occurs if declarer happens first to lead low to the Spade Queen. When East fails to follow, it's too late to recover and declarer falls short. A little more devotion will do it.

Caution: Missing J-10-x-x

A variation occurs when the four missing trumps are the J-10-x-x. You can protect yourself only against one opponent because you need two top honors over the defender with J-10-x-x. The safety play is to play the single honor first. Here's an example:

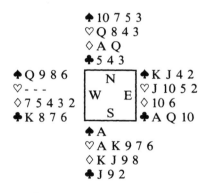

| ♠ 10 7 5 3 |
| ♡ Q 8 4 3 |
| ◇ A Q |
| ♣ 5 4 3 |

♠ Q 9 8 6   ♠ K J 4 2
♡ - - -   N   ♡ J 10 5 2
◇ 7 5 4 3 2 W E ◇ 10 6
♣ K 8 7 6   S   ♣ A Q 10

♠ A
♡ A K 9 7 6
◇ K J 9 8
♣ J 9 2

South	West	North	East
1 ♡	Pass	2 ♡	Pass
4 ♡	All Pass		

Opening lead, Club 6

East wins the Club Ace, cashes the Queen, and continues to West's King. West's next lead is a Diamond and dummy's Ace takes the trick.

Declarer is ready to pull trumps. Can you find the safest way to play them?

This time the safety play is to win the first trick with the single top honor, the Queen. If West holds the J-10-5-2, no play can prevent West from winning a trump trick because the 10 will force the Queen and then the Jack is a certain winner.

If East has J-10-5-2, declarer can pick them up because he has two top honors over East and can finesse twice toward the A-K-9-7.

In a capsule: When you're missing J-x-x-x (a single honor), lead one of the double honors first; when you're missing J-10-x-x (a double honor), lead the single honor first.

Caution: Missing Q-J-x-x

Let's try another safety play. Remember we're studying how to insure e-a-s-y contracts by playing cautiously.

```
              ♠ A 10 7
              ♡ A Q 7 6
              ◇ Q J 3 2
              ♣ 7 2
  ♠ Q J 3 2   ┌─────────┐   ♠ - - -
  ♡ 4 3       │    N    │   ♡ J 10 9 5 2
  ◇ 10 8 6    │ W     E │   ◇ 9 7 5
  ♣ Q J 5 4   │    S    │   ♣ 10 9 8 6 3
              └─────────┘
              ♠ K 9 8 6 5 4
              ♡ K 8
              ◇ A K 4
              ♣ A K
```

South	West	North	East
1 ♠	Pass	3 ♠	Pass
4 NT	Pass	5 ♡	Pass
6 ♠	All Pass		

Opening lead, Club Queen

You win the Club King, noting that you have no losers in Clubs or in Hearts or in Diamonds. You can bring in the little slam if you can hold your trump losers to one. Holding nine trumps, the hand looks like a cinch so you ask, "Can anything defeat me?"

There are four outstanding Spades and you mentally deal them every possible way. If they are divided 2-2, there are no losers at all; if they're 3-1, you'll probably lose one trick but that's all right. If they're 4-0, there is danger ahead. You could lose your little slam! Can you find a safety play to protect yourself against all four trumps in one hand?

| (1) | ♠ A 10 7 | (2) | ♠ A 10 7 |

♠ Q J 3 2   [N W E S]   ♠ - - -   ♠ - - -   [N W E S]   ♠ Q J 3 2

| | ♠ K 9 8 6 5 4 | | ♠ K 9 8 6 5 4 |

The safety play is to lead a low trump at trick two from the South hand. When West follows with a low card, insert the 7 spot. If East wins your problem is solved because the division is no worse than 3-1 and you can pick up the two remaining Spades with the Ace-King. If East fails to follow, the 7 wins. Since you still retain the Ace-King, you lose only one trick.

Suppose when you lead the Spade 4, West shows out. You rise with the Ace, lead the 10, and finesse East on the way back. If East covers with the Jack, you win the King and East never gets but one trick. If he doesn't cover, the 10 is a winner so you follow low. Now you play the 7 to the King and East still wins just one trick.

You play this way because you can afford to lose one trick and want to guarantee you won't lose two. If the opposing trumps happen to break 2-2, you surrender a trick you don't need to lose, but you do it to insure the contract. The premium you pay is 30 points above the line.

A casual player just leads to the Spade Ace. Anytime West holds four trumps, declarer has frittered away a slam.

If you were in 7 Spades, of course you couldn't afford a safety play. You have to play optimistically, hoping the opposing cards are divided, and cash a top Spade on the first round.

SCIENTIFIC PLAYS

The other type of safety play is the technical handling of certain combinations of honor cards to guard against devilish distribution.

Caution: Missing Q-10-x-x-x

There is a safety play to protect you when you have the precarious holding of A-K-9-x-x opposite J-8-x in a key suit. The following deal pictures the problem:

```
              ♠ Q J 3
              ♡ A Q J
              ◇ J 8 5
              ♣ A Q 4 2
  ♠ 8 6 4          N          ♠ 9 7 5
  ♡ 7 6                       ♡ 9 8 5 4 3
  ◇ Q 10 6 3    W     E       ◇ 2
  ♣ J 10 9 8       S          ♣ K 6 5 3
              ♠ A K 10 2
              ♡ K 10 2
              ◇ A K 9 7 4
              ♣ 7
```

South	West	North	East
1 ◇	Pass	3 NT	Pass
4 ♠	Pass	5 ◇	Pass
6 ◇	All Pass		

Opening lead, Club Jack

A quick reconnaissance reveals the only possible losers are in the trump suit. If the outstanding Diamonds split 3-2, any play will bring in the slam. Can you work out a maneuver that will limit the losses to one trick if the trumps are 4-1 with both honors in the long hand? There is a way!

(1)   ◇ J 8 5   (2)   ◇ J 8 5

◇ Q 10 6 3 | N W E S | ◇ 2   ◇ 2 | N W E S | ◇ Q 10 6 3

      ◇ A K 9 7 4   ◇ A K 9 7 4

When this hand arose the real declarer was an expert. Winning the Club Ace, he played a low trump to the Ace. Both opponents followed. Then he led a low Diamond from his hand toward dummy's Jack. This was a safety play that carried a 100% guarantee only one Diamond trick would be lost. It surrendered a Diamond on the second round and held either opponent to a single trick.

Here's how: if West holds Q-10-x-x as in (1), West can win the second round, but then dummy's Jack and declarer's King draw the rest. If West ducks it doesn't help him. Declarer plays the Jack and it wins. The King takes the next round, and West still wins only one trick.

If East began with the Q-10-x-x as in (2), the slam is likewise secure. In that event, West fails to follow on the second round and dummy's Jack forces the Queen. Declarer wins any return, reaches dummy with a Spade or Heart, and leads a Diamond through East's 10-6 toward his own K-9. Again he wraps up the suit with a single loss.

This was the technique: *He first played a top honor from the hand with two honors, retaining an honor card in each hand to stand guard over each side of the table.* Then he led toward the honor in the short hand.

Vary the Diamond suit some and we vary the safety play:

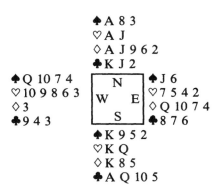

$\diamondsuit$ K 8 5

$\diamondsuit$ A J 9 6 2

First, count your tricks. If you can't afford to lose any Diamond tricks, you play just as you always have. Cash the King, lead toward the A-J, and finesse.

If you can afford to lose one trick, there is a safer way. The situation arose in this hand:

$\spadesuit$ A 8 3
$\heartsuit$ A J
$\diamondsuit$ A J 9 6 2
$\clubsuit$ K J 2

$\spadesuit$ Q 10 7 4 $\spadesuit$ J 6
$\heartsuit$ 10 9 8 6 3 $\heartsuit$ 7 5 4 2
$\diamondsuit$ 3 $\diamondsuit$ Q 10 7 4
$\clubsuit$ 9 4 3 $\clubsuit$ 8 7 6

$\spadesuit$ K 9 5 2
$\heartsuit$ K Q
$\diamondsuit$ K 8 5
$\clubsuit$ A Q 10 5

South	West	North	East
1 NT	Pass	6 NT	Pass
All Pass			

Opening lead, Heart 10

Declarer has ten tricks off the top — two Spades, two Hearts, two Diamonds, and four Clubs. He needs two more and has to find them in the Diamond suit.

If the missing Diamonds are divided 3-2 the slam rolls. Is there a way to protect against a 4-1 split with one opponent holding Q-10-x-x? Yes! There is a safety play that will insure the contract. Try to work it out from these layouts:

(1)   ◊ A J 9 6 2   (2)   ◊ A J 9 6 2

◊ 3 [W N E S] ◊ Q 10 7 4   ◊ Q 10 7 4 [W N E S] ◊ 3

       ◊ K 8 5   ◊ K 8 5

To lose no more than one trick, *first lay down the Ace, the top card in the hand with two honors.* Then lead a low Diamond toward the K-8 and cover whatever East plays. Suppose East inserts the 7; cover with the 8. Now, if West has a Diamond and can win the trick, there's a 3-2 split and you're safe. In (1), the 8 wins and the puzzle is solved. Next, cash the King and lose one trick.

What if West harbors the Q-10-x-x as in (2)? The safety play still is to cash the Ace, the top card in the hand with two honors. Then lead low toward the King. When East fails to follow, rise with the King and lead back toward North's J-9-6 through West's Q-10. This renders West helpless. He can win only one trick. If West plays low, you win the Jack and lose only one trick. If West takes the Queen, you play low. When you regain the lead, cross to the North hand with a Spade or a Club, and lead the Jack to clear the suit. Again, you lose only one trick.

If you play this combination the normal way and run into deal (1), you lose two tricks and your slam is dead — a slam that is easy as pie to make with a safety play.

The same principle applies if the Jack happens to be dealt to the South hand:

(3)   ◊ A 9 6 5 2   (4)   ◊ A 9 6 5 2

◊ 3 [W N E S] ◊ Q 10 7 4   ◊ Q 10 7 4 [W N E S] ◊ 3

       ◊ K J 8   ◊ K J 8

In (3) cash the King, *the top honor in the hand with two honors.* Cross to the North hand in another suit and lead a little Diamond toward the J-8 (the hand that is shorter). If East plays the 7, cover with the 8; if East plays the 10, put up the Jack. When West shows out, South wins. Now you still have the Ace to pick up one of East's cards, and you lose a single trick. If East should rise with the Queen, of course you play low and have the Jack and the Ace to clear the suit.

In (4) again you first win the King, cross to the North hand in another suit, and lead low toward the J-8. When East shows out, rise with the Jack to force the Queen. When you regain the lead, get in the South hand to lead through West's 10-7 toward North's A-9-6 and you still lose only one trick.

Remember, card combinations are treated differently depending on how many tricks you need. Here are the same cards dealt another way:

$$\diamondsuit A\ 9\ 5\ 4$$

```
        N
    W       E
        S
```

$$\diamondsuit K\ J\ 3\ 2$$

With this combination, suppose you need four tricks. Lead a low Diamond from North planning to finesse the Jack. This is right if East has Q-x-x, Q-x, or Q. Do not cash the Ace first. Even when East has the singleton Queen, four Diamond tricks are still available because North will have the A-9 over West's 10-8. If West holds the singleton Queen, four tricks never are available because East has 10-8-7-6.

However, if you need only three tricks, your contract is in the bag because there is a 100% technical play.

(5)	$\diamondsuit A\ 9\ 5\ 4$	(6)	$\diamondsuit A\ 9\ 5\ 4$
$\diamondsuit Q\ 10\ 8\ 7$	[W E] $\diamondsuit 6$	$\diamondsuit 6$	[W E] $\diamondsuit Q\ 10\ 8\ 7$
	$\diamondsuit K\ J\ 3\ 2$		$\diamondsuit K\ J\ 3\ 2$

First cash the King, *the big card in the hand with two honors.* Next, lead toward the North hand and cover West's card. You're planning to finesse the 9. However, if West shows out, as in (6), you go up with the Ace and lead back through East's Q-10 toward South's J-3, again losing only one trick.

Caution: Missing K-J-x-x

Let's look at a similar play based on the same principle. This time you're missing K-J-x-x.

The situation arises often. Here is one occasion from a rubber bridge game showing the dilemma that confronts a declarer:

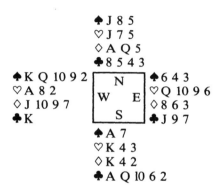

```
              ♠ J 8 5
              ♡ J 7 5
              ◇ A Q 5
              ♣ 8 5 4 3
♠ K Q 10 9 2    ┌─────┐    ♠ 6 4 3
♡ A 8 2         │  N  │    ♡ Q 10 9 6
◇ J 10 9 7    W │     │ E  ◇ 8 6 3
♣ K             │  S  │    ♣ J 9 7
                └─────┘
              ♠ A 7
              ♡ K 4 3
              ◇ K 4 2
              ♣ A Q 10 6 2
```

South	West	North	East
1 NT	Pass	2 NT	Pass
3 NT	All Pass		

Opening lead, Spade King

Since the King lead indicates West also holds the Queen, declarer wins the Ace. He is assured of two Spade tricks by later leading toward dummy's Jack. He counts two Spade tricks and three Diamonds, so he needs four Club tricks. He can afford to lose one Club trick but not two. Try to work out the safest possible play.

If you must take all the tricks, you play the cards as you need them to be. You make the normal play of leading from the North hand and finessing the Queen. You're playing East to hold the K-x and West to hold J-x.

When you require only four tricks, that's the wrong way. Suppose you did play that way and lost the first trick to the King. What would you do next?

(1) ♣9 7 5 4

♣K [N W E S] ♣J 6 2

♣A Q 10 8 3

(2) ♣9 7 5 4

♣K J [N W E S] ♣6 2

♣A Q 10 8 3

If you guess to play the Ace you might find the King had been a singleton, as in (1), and you have to lose a second trick to East's Jack. If, however, you decide to repeat the finesse, it is possible you'll lose to the Jack, as in (2). You have to guess and if you guess wrong you're lost.

The predicament can be resolved with a technical play that eliminates any guess. Cash the Ace first. Notice in (1) the safety play brings you a gift — the singleton King falls. In (2) the Jack falls. Either way your troubles are over.

What if only small cards fall? Now cross to dummy and lead toward the Q-10-8-3. If East follows, it has to be the King or Jack and the problem is solved. If East shows out, you lose two tricks, but nothing could have been done about it because West began with the K-J-x. The play of the Ace originally is a safety play that protects against every eventuality you can handle. It is the scientific play when you can afford to lose one trick.

Caution: Missing K-J-10-9-8

Can you unravel the safety play on this one? As usual, it's a skimpy trump suit — or it could be a long minor in your No Trump contract. What is the safest way to handle this holding to win four tricks?

♣7 6 5

[N W E S]

♣A Q 4 3 2

The normal play is to lead low from the North hand and finesse the Queen on the first round. This is entirely wrong! If you tried that way, work some more. Then look at these different deals:

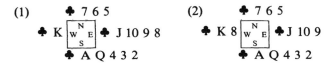

(1) ♣ 7 6 5
♣ K [N W E S] ♣ J 10 9 8
♣ A Q 4 3 2

(2) ♣ 7 6 5
♣ K 8 [N W E S] ♣ J 10 9
♣ A Q 4 3 2

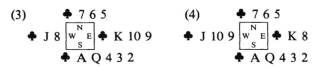

(3) ♣ 7 6 5
♣ J 8 [N W E S] ♣ K 10 9
♣ A Q 4 3 2

(4) ♣ 7 6 5
♣ J 10 9 [N W E S] ♣ K 8
♣ A Q 4 3 2

With the K-J-10-9-8 outstanding, South's two honors cannot possibly drop them all, so one trick must be lost. *The correct first play is to lay down the Ace.* This guards against the singleton King as in (1) and holds your losses to the fewest possible, two tricks.

In (2) nothing interesting appears on the Ace, so you cross to the North hand in another suit and lead toward the Queen. When East plays the 10, you have to guess. If you choose to play low, you hold your losses to one trick.

Deal (3) is similar. You have to guess. If you happen to play the Queen, you hold your losses to one trick.

In (4) on the second round the King appears, so you play low and hold your losses to one trick.

DRILL ON SAFETY PLAYS

(1) Can you guarantee this little slam?

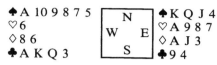

```
♠ A 10 9 8 7 5      ♠ K Q J 4
♡ 6             N    ♡ A 9 8 7
◊ 8 6         W   E  ◊ A J 3
♣ A K Q 3       S    ♣ 9 4
```

West	North	East	South
1 ♠	4 ♡	4 NT	Pass
5 ♡	Dbl.	6 ♠	

Opening lead, Heart King

(2) Against 6 Hearts, North leads the Club King. How would you play the hand? How would you play trumps?

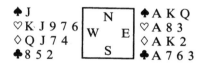

```
♠ J                 ♠ A K Q
♡ K J 9 7 6    N    ♡ A 8 3
◊ Q J 7 4    W   E  ◊ A K 2
♣ 8 5 2         S   ♣ A 7 6 3
```

(3) Against 7 Spades, North leads the Club Queen. Would you stake your life on the Grand after you, as West, win the first trick with the Club Ace?

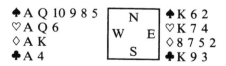

```
♠ A Q 10 9 8 5      ♠ K 6 2
♡ A Q 6        N    ♡ K 7 4
◊ A K        W   E  ◊ 8 7 5 2
♣ A 4           S   ♣ K 9 3
```

(4) Against West's 4 Spades, North leads the Diamond King. What is the safest way to play trumps?

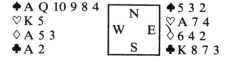

```
♠ A Q 10 9 8 4      ♠ 5 3 2
♡ K 5          N    ♡ A 7 4
◊ A 5 3      W   E  ◊ 6 4 2
♣ A 2           S   ♣ K 8 7 3
```

17. Give Clubs the Litmus Test

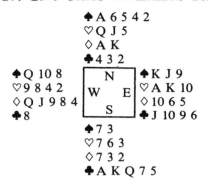

♠ A 6 5 4 2
♡ Q J 5
◇ A K
♣ 4 3 2

♠ Q 10 8   ♠ K J 9
♡ 9 8 4 2   ♡ A K 10
◇ Q J 9 8 4   ◇ 10 6 5
♣ 8   ♣ J 10 9 6

♠ 7 3
♡ 7 6 3
◇ 7 3 2
♣ A K Q 7 5

North deals
None vulnerable

North	East	South	West
1 ♠	Pass	1 NT	All Pass

Opening lead, Diamond Queen

West kicked off with the Diamond Queen and dummy's King won.

With six tricks ready to go — one Spade, two Diamonds, and three Clubs — the hand looked e-a-s-y. The long Club suit would bring in two more.

"My granddaughter could make this one," South cried with confidence. "I even have an overtrick."

Moving right along, he quite properly led a Club to the Queen. Then, alas, he cashed the King and West failed to follow. It was a cruel blow. South was back on square one with only the six tricks he started with, and that was all he ever got. Instead of accruing a little nest egg below the line, he handed the opponents 50 points.

When both defenders followed to the first Club trick, the contract was in the bag. The five outstanding Clubs were known then to be divided 4-1 or 3-2, so declarer's thoughts should be devoted to protecting against a 4-1 division. All he had to do was take the precautionary step of conceding the second round. East would win but could do no harm, and dummy still had a Club to reach the closed hand. This way the Clubs contributed four tricks and the contract rolled.

"Maybe you can persuade your granddaughter to teach you the safety play," dummy suggested and everybody laughed. Everybody except South.

A fine declarer attempts to shape his play so he can make his contract if the adverse cards are divided favorably or unfavorably. He hopes for the best but prepares for the worst. It is true South may lose 30 points by giving up the chance to make an overtrick, but this is a trifle compared with the safety of his contract.

18. Tuning in on the Bidding

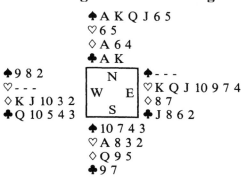

```
                    ♠ A K Q J 6 5
                    ♡ 6 5
                    ◇ A 6 4
                    ♣ A K
    ♠ 9 8 2              N          ♠ - - -
    ♡ - - -                         ♡ K Q J 10 9 7 4
    ◇ K J 10 3 2     W     E        ◇ 8 7
    ♣ Q 10 5 4 3         S          ♣ J 8 6 2
                    ♠ 10 7 4 3
                    ♡ A 8 3 2
                    ◇ Q 9 5
                    ♣ 9 7
```

East deals
North-South vulnerable

East	South	West	North
3 ♡	Pass	Pass	4 ♠
All Pass			

Opening lead, Heart King

East's preempt didn't leave much room for North-South to talk things over, so North, with nine winners in his own hand, took the bull by the horns and leaped to a Spade game. East led the Heart King.

Declarer was delighted with dummy. The Heart Ace gave him his tenth trick. Could any calamity befall him? Reflecting on the auction, he deduced East had a seven-carder. The six Hearts in his hand and dummy's accounted for the whole suit. West was void! Now the hand held no secrets.

Declarer ducked in dummy, West discarded the Diamond 3, and the Heart King won. East laid down the Heart Queen, dummy ducked again, and West played the Diamond 2.

Since declarer could now trump Hearts, East shifted to a Diamond. Declarer won the Ace and pulled all of West's trumps, carefully winding up in dummy. At last it was safe to put the Heart Ace on the table, and on it declarer tossed away a Diamond loser. He took ten tricks and scored his game, a fine reward for taking the time and trouble to visualize the Heart distribution.

Look at the milk that is spilt if North fails to analyze the bidding! In thoughtless haste he jumps on the Heart King with the Ace, West trumps, and North never recovers. He's down one.

Even without East's preempt, the duck is still the safety play that guarantees the game.

19. The Tried and True

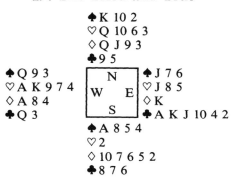

```
              ♠ K 10 2
              ♡ Q 10 6 3
              ◇ Q J 9 3
              ♣ 9 5
  ♠ Q 9 3          N        ♠ J 7 6
  ♡ A K 9 7 4               ♡ J 8 5
  ◇ A 8 4    W       E      ◇ K
  ♣ Q 3          S          ♣ A K J 10 4 2
              ♠ A 8 5 4
              ♡ 2
              ◇ 10 7 6 5 2
              ♣ 8 7 6
```

South deals
East-West vulnerable

South	West	North	East
Pass	1 ♡	Pass	2 ♣
Pass	2 NT	Pass	4 ♡
All Pass			

Opening lead, Diamond Queen

Facing two certain Spade losers, the problem that plagued declarer was how to play trumps to lose only a single trick. If the five missing cards were split 3-2, the contract was e-a-s-y. What if they were 4-1? That would require careful play and declarer proceeded to give it just that.

After winning the first trick with dummy's Diamond King, West cashed the Heart Ace. This left an honor in each hand to jockey with either opponent who might have started with Q-10-x-x. Next came a low Heart from his hand. North followed low, declarer flew up with dummy's Jack, and South showed out. (West plays so beautifully!)

Now the play was elementary. Declarer took the Heart King and surrendered a trump to North. The defenders grabbed their two Spades and were book-in but that was the end of the road for them. Declarer had a fistful of winners.

West's safety play of a low Heart toward the Jack on the second round of trumps works just as well if South has Q-10-x-x. In that event, North fails to follow and dummy's Jack forces the Queen. Declarer easily regains the lead, crosses to dummy with a Club to return a trump through South's 10-6 toward his own K-9, and still holds his trump losers to one.

If the outstanding trumps had been distributed 3-2, with the Queen doubleton, the safety play would have cost an overtrick. Any other set-up and it would cost nothing.

20. Don't Sleep at the Switch

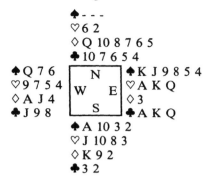

♠ - - -
♡ 6 2
♢ Q 10 8 7 6 5
♣ 10 7 6 5 4

♠ Q 7 6
♡ 9 7 5 4
♢ A J 4
♣ J 9 8

♠ K J 9 8 5 4
♡ A K Q
♢ 3
♣ A K Q

♠ A 10 3 2
♡ J 10 8 3
♢ K 9 2
♣ 3 2

West deals
All vulnerable

West	North	East	South
Pass	Pass	2 ♠	Pass
3 ♠	Pass	4 NT	Pass
5 ♢	Pass	6 ♠	All Pass

Opening lead, Heart Jack

With no losers in Hearts, Diamonds, or Clubs, the slam looks e-a-s-y. The trump Ace is a sure loser, and declarer's only worry is losing another trump trick. He captured trick one with the Heart Queen.

East planned to pull trumps immediately but paused to ponder the situation. If the four outstanding Spades were 2-2 or 3-1, he could play his honors any way and never lose but one trick. Since sometimes Fate deals them 4-0, declarer analyzed that threat. Then, carefully he laid down the Spade King. This was the safety play and kept an honor in each hand, the Queen in dummy and the Jack in his own hand, to protect against either adversary holding four. South ran up with the Ace and North was unable to follow suit. (He slyly discarded a black card hoping declarer wouldn't notice he didn't have a trump.)

Back came another Heart and declarer won the King. He next played the trump 4, South ducked, and declarer took the marked finesse. Dummy's 7 won.

It was routine to pick up South's other trumps. Next came the Spade Queen; dummy's Diamond Ace was cashed and a Diamond ruffed. Now East's Spade Jack brought down the Spade 10 and declarer claimed the slam.

The safety play of first leading one of the honors from the hand with two honors works also if all the trumps are bunched in the North hand. In that event, after North captures the Spade King with the Ace, declarer wins any return, plays a Spade to dummy's Queen, and continues with dummy's last Spade, finessing through North's 10-3 toward his own K-9.

The trap to avoid is playing dummy's Spade Queen on the first round of trumps. With no honor left on that side of the table to stand guard over South, no power on earth can prevent South from winning two trumps because his A-10-3 hover over declarer's K-J-9-8-5.

VI. THE ART OF COUNTING

If you want to improve your bridge by leaps and bounds, learn to count the original distribution in the hand of one opponent, the cards he held during the bidding. It'll give you a clairvoyance that will enable you to drop singleton Kings, to catch Queens, and to guess which opponent holds an all important Jack.

Counting isn't difficult once you get the hang of it. The biggest hurdle is to convince yourself you can do it. You can count trumps, can't you? You've often counted your next best suit, haven't you? Just take on one more. When you know the distribution of three suits you can deduce the division of the fourth. As you practice it will get easier. When you learn to do this you're approaching the expert arena.

How to Count a Suit

Some players count a suit in a rather clumsy fashion that forces them to keep recounting. The easiest way is to add your cards to dummy's and subtract the total from 13. That gives you the number the other two players have. This is the number you use for the rest of your counting.

To illustrate: you hold A-K-9-4-2 of trumps and dummy has Q-8-6-3. Your mental exercise is, "I have five, dummy has four, the opponents have four. Theirs are divided 4-0, 3-1, or 2-2."

You draw one round of trumps. Everybody follows. (No counting to do yet.) You draw another round and West shows out. Now, count, basing it on the fact the opponents started with four trumps. "Ah-ha," you muse. "Trumps were 3-1. East began with three and still has one left."

This method starts you thinking about one opponents' original 13 cards and that is the picture you want. When you discover the original distribution of one opponent's hand, you can deduce whatever you want to know about the other opponent's hand.

Let's try a hand together.

♠ 7 5 3
♡ A Q 4
◇ A J 10
♣ A J 8 2

♠ 4
♡ K J 10 7 6 2
◇ K Q 3
♣ K 10 9

East-West vulnerable

West	North	East	South
3 ♠	Double	Pass	4 NT
Pass	5 ♠	Pass	6 ♡
All Pass			

Opening lead, Spade King

After bidding boldly, it was now up to South to play brilliantly. He spotted 11 ready-made tricks — six Hearts, three Diamonds, and two Clubs. Turning the twelfth was a tantalizing problem because he had to finesse for the Club Queen and he could take it in either direction.

He wanted something more to go on than a lucky guess, so he set out to learn all he could about the Club suit. The clues would come from a study of the other suits, so he began to research the distribution of Spades, Hearts, and Diamonds.

West won the first trick with the Spade King and continued the Spade Ace. Declarer ruffed and led a small trump to dummy's Queen. Then he came off the board with a Spade. East was unable to follow and declarer ruffed. (Spades mental note: we had four; they had nine.) This trick disclosed that East started with exactly two Spades and *West started with seven Spades*. Declarer suspected this on the auction. Now that suspicion was confirmed.

South continued to pull trumps and on the second round East failed to follow. (Hearts mental note: we had nine, they had four.) Since East had been dealt only one of the opponents' four trumps, South easily deduced *West began with three Hearts.* Now South knew 10 of West's original cards, seven Spades and three Hearts.

South extracted West's last Heart, and pursued his detective work by playing three rounds of Diamonds. West followed on the first and second rounds but on the third was unable to follow. *Therefore, West began with two Diamonds.*

Now declarer knew for an absolute certainty the exact distribution of West's original 13 cards. *West was dealt seven Spades, three Hearts, two Diamonds, and the one card left had to be a Club.*

Consequently, South led a low Club from his hand to dummy's Ace and returned a little Club from dummy. When East played low, declarer finessed the 10 without a worry. He knew West had no more Clubs and the slam was coming in.

The whole hand was:

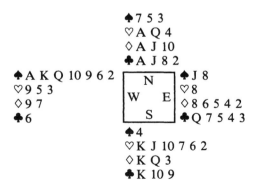

```
              ♠ 7 5 3
              ♡ A Q 4
              ◇ A J 10
              ♣ A J 8 2
♠ A K Q 10 9 6 2   ┌─────┐   ♠ J 8
♡ 9 5 3            │  N  │   ♡ 8
◇ 9 7           W  │     │  E  ◇ 8 6 5 4 2
♣ 6               │  S  │   ♣ Q 7 5 4 3
                   └─────┘
              ♠ 4
              ♡ K J 10 7 6 2
              ◇ K Q 3
              ♣ K 10 9
```

There is a technique which simplifies counting and we utilized it on this hand.

How To Count

1. Count the distribution of only one of the unseen hands. You see your hand and dummy's; there are two hands you can't see. Just count one of them. From these facts you deduce whatever you want to know about the other hand.

2. Count the hand you know the most about. We counted the West hand because we began knowing seven of his cards were Spades.

3. Systematically count one suit at a time. Begin counting when someone shows out. First we counted Spades when East showed out; next we counted Hearts when East showed out; then we checked out Diamonds when West failed to follow.

4. Play the suits you aren't worried about before you approach the suit you're worried about. Notice South played Spades, Hearts, and Diamonds — the three suits in which he had no worries — to learn all he could about the secrets of the hand before he tackled the worrisome Clubs.

Here's one to practice on. If you'd like to test your skills, write in the East-West distribution as it is revealed.

```
          ♠ A K Q
          ♡ 7 5 3
          ◇ K 10 4 2
          ♣ A J 5
        ┌─────────┐
        │    N    │
        │ W     E │
        │    S    │
        └─────────┘
          ♠ J 10 4
          ♡ A J
          ◇ A J 8 7 5
          ♣ K Q 3
```

South	West	North	East
1 NT	2 ♡	4 ♣	Pass
4 ♠	Pass	6 NT	All Pass

Opening lead, Heart King

West led the Heart King and South stopped to study. He saw the little slam was safe if he could locate the Diamond Queen. He also saw he was down a zillion if he misguessed because the defenders would quickly snap up all their Hearts.

If the four outstanding Diamonds were split 2-2 there was no hunting at all. However, the percentages favored a 3-1 split. If that were the case, he'd have to finesse and he could finesse either way.

Like a good detective, he started looking for clues right away. He ducked the first Heart! It was a strange play, but there was a motive behind it — to help him learn more about the Heart suit.

West pursued with the Heart Queen and East showed out as declarer won the Ace. *Clue 1: West began with seven Hearts.*

Next, he played all his Club winners. West could follow only twice. *Clue 2: West started with only two Clubs.*

Then he played another suit he wasn't worried about, Spades, laying down the A-K-Q in rapid succession. West followed only twice. *Clue 3: West started with two Spades.*

Now West's original distribution was proven — seven Hearts, two Clubs, and two Spades. His other two cards had to be Diamonds, so the suit was split 2-2. This knowledge was very important because, without it, declarer might have reasoned that since West had so many Hearts, he didn't have many Diamonds. Proceeding on this premise, declarer might have been tempted to play the odds and finesse East for the Diamond Queen instead of playing for the drop.

With confidence South cashed the Ace and King of Diamonds, snaring the Queen. It wasn't a guess and it wasn't luck. It was skill.

The whole hand was:

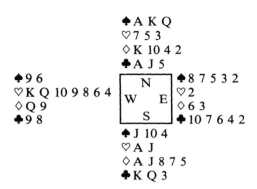

♠ A K Q
♡ 7 5 3
◇ K 10 4 2
♣ A J 5

♠ 9 6
♡ K Q 10 9 8 6 4
◇ Q 9
♣ 9 8

♠ 8 7 5 3 2
♡ 2
◇ 6 3
♣ 10 7 6 4 2

♠ J 10 4
♡ A J
◇ A J 8 7 5
♣ K Q 3

Here's another hand where locating the Queen would bring in a contract.

♠ A Q 7 2
♡ K J 10
◇ 8 6 4
♣ A 9 4

♠ K J 10 9 6
♡ A 7 5
◇ J 7 5
♣ K 3

South	West	North	East
1 ♠	2 ◇	3 ♠	Pass
4 ♠	All Pass		

Opening lead, Diamond King

Declarer helplessly followed suit to three rounds of Diamonds, the opponents had their book, and declarer still faced a possible Heart loser. Since he didn't relish risking his contract by guessing who had the Heart Queen, he began a search for clues.

East followed only to the first round of Diamonds. *Clue 1: West had six Diamonds.* Since declarer already knew almost half of West's cards, that's the hand he counted.

At trick four West shifted to the Club Queen. South won the King. If you were South how would you proceed? Which suit would you lead next? After that which suit?

The real South extracted trumps and they all fell in two rounds. *Clue 2: West had two Spades.* Declarer had systematically counted two suits.

Next, checking out Clubs, declarer played over to the Ace and ruffed a Club on the way back. West followed. *Clue 3: West had at least three Clubs.*

There were two unknown cards in West's hand. Either both were Hearts, or one was a Heart and one a Club. Since there were seven Hearts out, declarer knew East had at least five Hearts. Consequently, East had five chances to be dealt the Queen and West only two chances, so declarer made the percentage play. He led a low Heart to the King and returned the Jack, taking the two-way finesse against East. It won and he had his ten tricks.

The whole hand was:

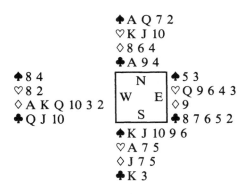

Go With the Odds

Whenever a declarer cannot pinpoint the location of a missing honor, his next best bet is to go with the odds. The law of probability states that the player who has the greater number of cards in a suit is more likely to have a specific card.

If the Hearts in the East-West hands were removed, shuffled, and redealt 100 times, giving five to East and two to West, East would get the Queen 71.5 times and West 28.5, so your play will win approximately 71% of the time and lose approximately 28% of the time.

Even if the suit were split 4-3, you improve your chances by putting the Queen in the hand with four cards.

It is said that an expert can locate a missing Queen eight times out of ten! This is the way he goes about it. You, too, can make lucrative plays if you care enough to reckon how many cards an opponent holds in a suit.

The sources of counting clues are the bidding, the opening lead, and the play as it progresses.

The Auction Tells a Story

Listening to the auction gives clues when you think about what bids mean.

West opens 3 Hearts. How many Hearts does he have? Probably seven. Remember that when the play begins because you know more than half his cards. What if he opens 4 Hearts? He probably has eight. How about an opening 1 Heart? Probably five Hearts, but listen to his next call. It might contain another counting clue.

(1)   1 ♡ ⊞ 1 NT   (2)   1 ♡ ⊞ 1 ♠
        2 ♡   2 ♣

        (3)   1 ♡ ⊞ 1 NT
                2 ♣   2 ♡
                3 ♣

In auction (1) West rebid Hearts showing a six-card suit and you place almost half his cards. In (2) West's bid of a new suit is almost always a four-carder, so you know nine of his cards — five Hearts and four Clubs. In (3) West rebid his second suit showing five Clubs, so assume he has five Hearts and five Clubs although he could have six Hearts and five Clubs. *When West rebids his second suit he emphasizes the length of his first suit.*

(4)   1♣   1◇   (5)   1♣   1♡
     1 NT   1♣   2♣
                                2♡

(6)   1 NT   2♣
     2◇   2♡
     2 NT

Minor suit openings do not disclose as much about distribution. In (4) when West rebid 1 No Trump, jumping over both majors, West denied holding four Hearts or four Spades. He has even distribution. Unless he's a very unusual bidder, he doesn't have a singleton and he has only one doubleton, so assume for now he's 3-3-2-5 or 3-3-3-4.

In (5) West's rebid of 1 Spade shows four Spades and his delayed Heart raise shows three Hearts. Whenever a player bids three suits he's obviously short in the fourth suit. He probably has 4-3-2-4 or 4-3-1-5.

An opening No Trump promises a balanced distribution of 4-3-3-3, 4-4-3-2, or 5-3-3-2, but sometimes an auction pinpoints it even more. In (6) East employs Stayman and West responds 2 Diamonds saying he has no four-card major, so you start thinking he might be 3-3-4-3 or 3-3-3-4. But wait. East now bids Hearts to show he holds five Hearts and West repeats his No Trump bid. Obviously, West has only a doubleton Heart. Consequently you mentally re-arrange his distribution. He *specifically* has three Spades and two Hearts. His other eight cards are in the minors and they're 4-4 or 5-3.

Since you get to see your own hand and dummy, once you know declarer's distribution you can deduce partner's distribution.

The Lead Tells a Story

Opening leads are standardized. They mean something and sometimes they draw a blueprint of a whole hand. You can read the map when they spread it out in front of you.

The most often led card in bridge is fourth-best. When the lead comes down, analyze it. By studying your hand and dummy you usually can figure out what it is. The lowest of four? Fourth from a five-card suit? Top of a doubleton? A singleton?

If it is an honor, say the King, the leader is marked with the Queen or the Ace. Looking at your hand and dummy you can usually tell which. When the Ace-King of a suit are outstanding and the suit isn't led, either the honors are divided or the other adversary holds both. This is also true of a missing King-Queen-Jack.

There are times when you'd like to know not only how many cards an opponent holds in a suit, but *which* cards.

Once you're feeling secure counting the distribution it's time to take on another kind of counting — points. It's a giant step. Try it after you're steady on your feet counting the distribution.

Counting Points

You can sometimes see through the backs of the opponents' cards, learning who holds a specific face card, by analyzing the bidding. It is easy to do when one opponent opens the bidding and you and your partner wind up in a game contract.

The first step is to add your points to dummy's. Let's say you have 15 and dummy 11. That totals 26 points. Then subtract that from 40, the total in the deck. There are only 14 oustanding points; they're all with the bidder except maybe a straggling Jack. Could be a Queen. But you know where the Aces and Kings are.

The point-count system is extremely helpful to a partnership in reaching the optimum contract. Bidders try to tell their partners the truth about their values. While they're telling their partners, they're also telling the defenders. However, most people are so drowsy while defending they fail to utilize that knowledge.

When a player opens 1 No Trump to tell his partner his hand values 16-18, he tells everybody else. Defenders who listen and add can make amazing leads.

Seven + Seven + Four = Eighteen

Opening No Trump bids are almost always a mirror that will reveal missing honors. Here's an example:

```
            ♠ J 3 2
            ♡ 10 8 4
            ◇ J 7 5
            ♣ A J 8 6
          ┌─────────┐
          │    N    │
          │ W     E │
          │    S    │
          └─────────┘
            ♠ 8 4
            ♡ K Q J 9 7 5
            ◇ 6 4
            ♣ K 10 7
```

West	North	East	South
1 NT	Pass	Pass	2 ♡
All Pass			

Opening lead, Diamond King

West tees off with the Diamond King, East signaling with the 8 for a continuation. West complies with the Diamond Ace and another Diamond. East covers dummy's Jack with the Queen and declarer trumps. *Clue 1: seven of West's points are the A-K of Diamonds.*

Declarer leads the trump King and West takes the Ace. *Clue 2: four of West's points are the trump Ace.*

West brings out the King-Ace of Spades, and again East asks for a continuation. West plays a third round of Spades, East playing the Queen and declarer ruffing. *Clue 3: West has seven points in Spades.*

Pulling another round of trumps, South finds a 2-2 split. Then he pauses to reflect. He has lost five tricks and he can't lose any more. He has to figure out who has the Club Queen.

Seat yourself in the South chair. Who has the dark-haired lady? All the clues are out.

West has shown up with 18 points — the A-K of Diamonds, the A-K of Spades, and the Ace of Hearts. He couldn't have the Queen of Clubs because then he'd have 20 points and that's over the limit for an opening bid of 1 No Trump.

Declarer finesses East for the missing Queen and the contract rolls.

On this hand it was very simple to count West's points. But if you had neglected to do so you might say, "There is only one missing Club honor and the No Trump bidder must have it," finesse the wrong way, and go down. When you counted West's points, you found it was impossible for him to hold a Club honor.

Counting distribution on this hand would not have helped you but counting points led you right to the Queen of Clubs. The whole hand was:

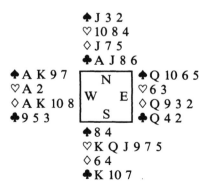

```
              ♠ J 3 2
              ♡ 10 8 4
              ◇ J 7 5
              ♣ A J 8 6
♠ A K 9 7    ┌─────────┐   ♠ Q 10 6 5
♡ A 2        │    N    │   ♡ 6 3
◇ A K 10 8   │ W     E │   ◇ Q 9 3 2
♣ 9 5 3      │    S    │   ♣ Q 4 2
             └─────────┘
              ♠ 8 4
              ♡ K Q J 9 7 5
              ◇ 6 4
              ♣ K 10 7
```

Counting points can help a defender see across the table into his partner's hand. On this next hand you're East and the auction tells you a story. Listen and be a hero.

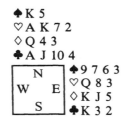

♠ K 5
♡ A K 7 2
◇ Q 4 3
♣ A J 10 4

♠ 9 7 6 3
♡ Q 8 3
◇ K J 5
♣ K 3 2

North	East	South	West
1 NT	Pass	2 ♡	All Pass

West led the Spade Queen and dummy's King won the trick. Declarer cashed the A-K of Hearts, crossed to the closed hand with the Spade Ace and led the Club Queen. You won the Club King and cashed the Heart Queen.

What now? Are you going to lead a Spade which declarer will ruff in dummy? Are you going to lead a Club? All dummy's Clubs are winners. Are you going to lead a Diamond away from your K-J? If declarer has the Diamond Ace, you'd be giving him a soft trick with dummy's Queen. But if your partner has the Diamond Ace, you might take three Diamond tricks before declarer throws Diamond losers on Clubs.

Who has the Diamond Ace? Declarer has shown up with the Spade Ace, the Club Queen, and is known to have the Heart Jack. That's seven points. It's impossible for South to have the Diamond Ace! He would have 11 points and would be playing a game contract.

In a second you are going to lay a little Diamond on the table and will soon see partner climb up with the Ace and return a Diamond through dummy's Queen into your K-J and hold declarer to eight tricks; any other return would allow him to make ten. The whole hand was:

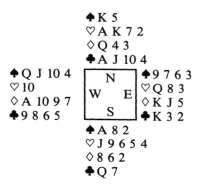

♠ K 5
♡ A K 7 2
◇ Q 4 3
♣ A J 10 4

♠ Q J 10 4
♡ 10
◇ A 10 9 7
♣ 9 8 6 5

♠ 9 7 6 3
♡ Q 8 3
◇ K J 5
♣ K 3 2

♠ A 8 2
♡ J 9 6 5 4
◇ 8 6 2
♣ Q 7

Defending is much more fun if you spend your time reading inferences instead of following suit woodenly and daydreaming. Here's a hand where East found a clue in the opening lead that helped him crack the case and send South's 1 No Trump down the river. This one is more advanced, but it illustrates how a defender can gather information.

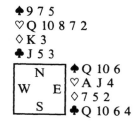

♠ 9 7 5
♡ Q 10 8 7 2
◇ K 3
♣ J 5 3

♠ Q 10 6
♡ A J 4
◇ 7 5 2
♣ Q 10 6 4

South	West	North	East
1 ◇	Pass	1 ♡	Pass
1 NT	All Pass		

Opening lead: Club 2

Sitting in the East seat, your assignment is to learn South's distribution. Based on the bidding and the opening lead, what can you deduce?

When West starts hostilities with the Club 2, you immediately know the division of the Club suit around the table. It indubitably is partner's fourth-best card and he has precisely four cards in the suit. Adding your four Clubs to dummy's three, you easily establish declarer has two Clubs.

South's rebid of 1 No Trump furnishes more clues. He has even distribution, yes, but just what? Since he couldn't raise Hearts, he has fewer than four Hearts. Since he didn't bid Spades, he has fewer than four Spades. A hand with even distribution contains only one doubleton. Therefore, South's hand probably is 3-3-5-2.

Next, throw your spotlight on South's high cards, the next mystery to solve. His bidding disclosed 13 to 15 points:

$$
\begin{array}{ll}
\text{Declarer} & = 13 \text{ to } 15 \\
\text{Dummy} & = 6 \\
\text{You} & = \underline{9} \\
& 28 \text{ to } 30
\end{array}
$$

Therefore, partner has 10 to 12 points. Where are they?

At trick one declarer plays dummy's Club Jack, you cover with the Queen, and South wins the Ace. *Declarer has four points in Clubs.*

Next he plays a Diamond to the King, returns a Diamond to his Queen, plays the Diamond Jack, and West wins the Ace. *Declarer has three points in Diamonds.*

Partner takes the Club King, the Club 9, and then gives you the Club 10. This is the fourth trick for your side. Which suit should you attack, Hearts or Spades? Looking for another clue you begin wondering what Spades partner has. Then the fog lifts. All this counting has given you high visibility. There are 13 cards in the Spade suit so, of course, partner has four Spades. Why did he attack with his four-card minor, K-9-8-2 of Clubs, instead of his four-card major? Because his minor was stronger!

Therefore, West does not have the Ace or King of Spades and declarer has both. *Declarer has seven points in Spades.* You know 14 of South's points. He could not have the Heart King because that would give him 17 points and he would have opened a No Trump. West has the Heart King.

You lay down a low Heart and partner wins his King (as you knew he would) and returns the suit through dummy's Q-10 to your A-J, and you reel off seven consecutive tricks, grabbing your Clubs and Hearts before declarer can seize his seven tricks in Diamonds and Spades.

This information was gleaned from a perfectly ordinary opening lead and an accurate interpretation of the auction. The complete hand was:

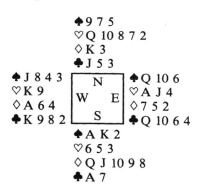

♠ 9 7 5
♡ Q 10 8 7 2
◇ K 3
♣ J 5 3

♠ J 8 4 3　　　♠ Q 10 6
♡ K 9　　　　 ♡ A J 4
◇ A 6 4　　　 ◇ 7 5 2
♣ K 9 8 2　　 ♣ Q 10 6 4

♠ A K 2
♡ 6 5 3
◇ Q J 10 9 8
♣ A 7

Tip

A good time to practice counting is when you're dummy. You can see only one hand so it is tougher. Try to count the distribution in declarer's hand or in one defender's hand. It's a good training period.

Counting Drill

(1) You're West playing 5 Diamonds:

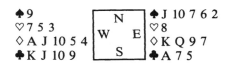

	♠ 9		
	♡ 7 5 3		
	◇ A J 10 5 4		
	♣ K J 10 9		

East side:
♠ J 10 7 6 2
♡ 8
◇ K Q 9 7
♣ A 7 5

North	East	South	West
1 ♠	Pass	1 NT	Pass
2 ♡	Pass	Pass	3 ◇
3 ♡	4 ◇	4 ♡	5 ◇

North led the Spade King and continued the Ace. You ruffed and pulled trumps, Diamonds falling 2-2. What do you know about the distribution of the Club suit? Can you make the contract?

(2) You're North on lead after this auction:

West	East	You hold:	♠ 9 4
1 ♣	1 ♡		♡ 8 6 4
2 NT	3 NT		◇ 9 5 2
			♣ 10 7 5 3 2

How many high-card points does West have? East? Your partner? What's your opening lead? Why?

(3) You're West playing 4 Hearts:

	♠ Q		
	♡ Q10 9 8 7 5		
	◇ A 10 9 5		
	♣ 7 3		

East side:
♠ A 9 7 4
♡ A J 4 3
◇ Q J 4
♣ J 5

East	South	West	North
1 ◇	1 NT	2 ♡	Pass
3 ♡	Pass	4 ♡	All Pass

North led the Club 2. South won the Ace and shot back a Club to North's King. Then North switched to a Spade.

Who has the Spade King? The Diamond King? The Heart King? How many tricks are you going to take?

21. Every Player Is Dealt 13 Cards

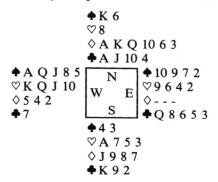

```
                    ♠ K 6
                    ♡ 8
                    ◊ A K Q 10 6 3
                    ♣ A J 10 4
  ♠ A Q J 8 5    ┌─────────┐    ♠ 10 9 7 2
  ♡ K Q J 10     │    N    │    ♡ 9 6 4 2
  ◊ 5 4 2        │ W     E │    ◊ - - -
  ♣ 7            │    S    │    ♣ Q 8 6 5 3
                 └─────────┘
                    ♠ 4 3
                    ♡ A 7 5 3
                    ◊ J 9 8 7
                    ♣ K 9 2
```

North deals
North-South vulnerable

North	East	South	West
1 ◊	Pass	1 ♡	1 ♠
3 ♣	Pass	3 ◊	Pass
4 NT	Pass	5 ◊	Pass
6 ◊	All Pass		

Opening lead, Spade 10

West's Spade bid, though well fortified, spurred North onward. Convinced his Spade King was favorably located, North plunged into a small slam.

East opened the Spade 10 and, sure enough, West won with the Spade Ace, establishing declarer's King. West shot back the Heart King and dummy's Ace won.

So far so good! But declarer still had a problem. He had to locate the Club Queen. He had a two-way finesse, so if he could figure out who held that crucial card he could trap the Queen and make the slam.

Did West have the Queen? West overcalled and East passed throughout. West should have most or maybe all of the outstanding honor cards. Yet it was still in the realm of possibility for East to hold the Queen. Swinging back and forth above North's head was this Damoclean sword threatening his 750 slam and 700 rubber.

North decided to sift through all the evidence he could possibly find before he committed himself to the crucial Club play. He could look for clues in the distribution of the other suits.

Winning the Heart Ace, he led a second Heart and ruffed with the Diamond Ace. He crossed back to dummy with a trump to the 7. East was unable to follow. *Clue 1: West held three Diamonds.*

Coming off dummy with a third round of Hearts, North trumped with the Diamond King and crossed back to dummy with a trump to the 8. Now he led dummy's fourth and last Heart, ruffing with the Diamond Queen. Both opponents followed. *Clue 2: West began with four Hearts.*

North pulled the last trump and reflected. He believed he knew 12 of West's original cards. The play proved West began with three Diamonds and four Hearts, and the bidding indicated he started with five or six Spades. If he started with five Spades he had room for one Club; if he started with six Spades he had no Clubs.

Playing fast and confidently now, North cashed his Club Ace and watched West follow suit with his only Club. Then he led the Club 4 and finessed the 9, barely blinking when it won. He cashed dummy's Club King. Returning to his own hand with the Spade King, declarer led his last Club, West covered, but dummy trumped. It was all over except writing down the big score.

22. Open Sesame!

By Baltimore's teacher, Becky Levering

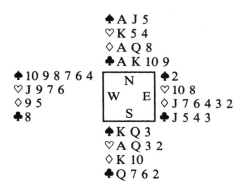

```
                    ♠ A J 5
                    ♡ K 5 4
                    ◊ A Q 8
                    ♣ A K 10 9
    ♠ 10 9 8 7 6 4      ┌─────┐      ♠ 2
    ♡ J 9 7 6        N  │     │      ♡ 10 8
    ◊ 9 5         W     │  E  │      ◊ J 7 6 4 3 2
    ♣ 8              S  │     │      ♣ J 5 4 3
                       └─────┘
                    ♠ K Q 3
                    ♡ A Q 3 2
                    ◊ K 10
                    ♣ Q 7 6 2
```

East deals
East-West vulnerable

East	South	West	North
Pass	1 NT	Pass	7 NT
All Pass			

Opening lead, Spade 10

After West led a Spade, South paused a moment. Twelve sure tricks were in view with Aces, Kings, and Queens. The battle was for the thirteenth and it could come from Clubs or Hearts. If the five outstanding Clubs split 3-2, the slam was easy; the danger was the possibility Clubs were 4-1 or 5-0. Even then he could rescue the grand slam with a finesse which was available through either opponent.

Another chance was the long Heart in his own hand. If that suit was divided 3-3, he could win the thirteenth trick with the extra Heart. With these two thoughts he proceeded to play.

Winning the opening lead with the Spade Queen, declarer tested Hearts, cashing the Ace-King-Queen. On the third round East couldn't follow. This was disappointing but he learned something. *Clue 1: West started with four Hearts.* Now the only chance was Clubs, so he decided to ferret out facts about the distribution of that crucial suit by first playing Spades and Diamonds.

He laid down the Spade Ace and East was unable to follow. *Clue 2: West started with six Spades.*

He took his other Spade winner and then moved to the Diamond suit, cashing the King-Ace-Queen, in that order. On the third round West couldn't follow. *Clue 3: West started with two Diamonds.*

All these plays were designed to compel the defenders to disclose their distribution, and at this point declarer had a complete count of West's original 13 cards. He began with exactly six Spades, four Hearts, two Diamonds, and, therefore, specifically one Club. This revealed there were four Clubs in the East hand.

Declarer led a Club to dummy's King and cashed the Ace. West couldn't follow suit! Now the grand slam was in South's hip pocket. He led the Club 10, finessed, and finished with thirteen tricks.

Let's suppose early in the hand declarer started on Clubs, as many players would. After all, that was his longest suit. Say he took the King, then the Queen. He would learn too late East had four to the Jack. Then when he tried Hearts and West turned up with four to the Jack, declarer would blame a cruel Fate.

It would be a stroke of bad luck, but Fate wouldn't be the only culprit! Careless play would be responsible, too.

Counting was the magic that opened the door to the treasure.

23. There are 40 Points in the Deck

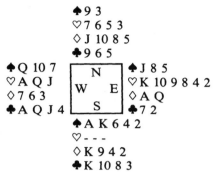

♠ 9 3
♡ 7 6 5 3
◊ J 10 8 5
♣ 9 6 5

♠ Q 10 7
♡ A Q J
◊ 7 6 3
♣ A Q J 4

♠ J 8 5
♡ K 10 9 8 4 2
◊ A Q
♣ 7 2

♠ A K 6 4 2
♡ - - -
◊ K 9 4 2
♣ K 10 8 3

South deals
All vulnerable

South	West	North	East
1 Spade	1 NT	Pass	4 Hearts
All Pass			

Opening lead, Spade King

On South's opening Spade King, North signaled with the 9. When South laid down the Spade Ace, North completed the echo with the 3. The Spade 6 was next and North ruffed. He made the obvious return of the Diamond Jack.

Playing like a man who knew what he was doing, declarer ran up with the Diamond Ace — refusing that finesse — and then led a Club and finessed the Jack. The Jack won.

He cashed the trump Ace, the Queen, and then played the Jack, overtaking in his hand with the King. He repeated the Club finesse, again winning and cashed the Club Ace. On this trick he threw away the Diamond Queen. Thus he took ten tricks — six Hearts, three Clubs, and one Diamond.

If declarer had taken a Diamond finesse at trick four he would have gone down before he ever gained the lead.

How did East know to spurn the Diamond finesse and rely on the Club finesse instead? Did he get a peek in South's hand? No! He paused to do some simple arithmetic and learned how to play the rest of the hand.

When he added his points to dummy's, he found 26. North produced the Diamond Jack to make 27. Since there are exactly 40 points in the deck, South must have the rest for his opening bid to make sense. He must hold the Club King and the Diamond King.

Declarer simply refused a finesse that was sure to lose and banked on a finesse that was sure to win.

24. An Educated Guess

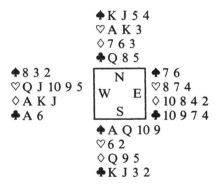

♠ K J 5 4
♡ A K 3
◇ 7 6 3
♣ Q 8 5

♠ 8 3 2
♡ Q J 10 9 5
◇ A K J
♣ A 6

♠ 7 6
♡ 8 7 4
◇ 10 8 4 2
♣ 10 9 7 4

♠ A Q 10 9
♡ 6 2
◇ Q 9 5
♣ K J 3 2

West deals
None vulnerable

West	North	East	South
1 ♡	Double	Pass	4 ♠
All Pass			

Opening lead, Diamond King

West won the Diamond King then switched to the Heart Queen and dummy's King captured the trick.

Pausing to analyze the hand, declarer counted three Diamond losers and one Club loser. That was one too many.

If Clubs were 3-3 (35% chance), his fourth Club would be established and he could throw one of dummy's Diamonds on it. What if the Clubs were split 4-2 (45% chance)? Undoubtedly the distribution of the Clubs was the problem to solve.

Extracting trumps in three rounds, South wound up in the closed hand. He led the Club deuce, West played low, and dummy's Queen won. This convinced South of something he had surmised from the auction, that West held the Club Ace.

Declarer stopped to see if he could figure out how many Clubs West had. He counted suit by suit. For his opening bid, West certainly held five Hearts. He had followed to three rounds of trumps. The opening lead of the Diamond King indicated West also held the Ace. Holding the Ace-King doubleton, it's customary to play the Ace first and then the King. Since West played the King first he must hold three Diamonds.

Now declarer believed he knew twelve of West's cards — five Hearts, three Spades, and three Diamonds, and the Club he had already played. The secret was out. He had started with only two Clubs, and the remaining one was the Ace.

Declarer came off dummy with the Club 5, East covered with the 7, and declarer contributed the 3. West, perforce, played his Ace and it fell "on air."

West led a Heart and dummy's Ace won. Declarer led another Heart and ruffed in his hand. Then he cashed the K-J of Clubs, dropping a Diamond from dummy. Since dummy still had a trump, declarer was able to ruff one Diamond loser and get ten tricks. He lost only two Diamonds and one Club.

Back up a bit and suppose for a moment South hadn't stopped to count the distribution. Suppose he covered East's Club 7 with the Jack. West, of course, would win the Ace just as he did. But now East would wind up with fourth-round control, so South would have to ruff his last Club, eventually losing tricks to West's Ace and Jack of Diamonds. Down one.

VII. THE ENDPLAY

The endplay is the act of throwing an opponent into the lead at that propitious moment when any card he returns gives away a trick. It is the most interesting of all the advanced plays. It's one of the thrills of the game.

Here's an endplay with only three cards remaining:

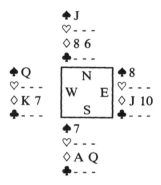

South is playing a small slam against which West opened the Spade King. South cashed 10 winners and now requires two of the three remaining tricks. The commonplace play is to finesse for the Diamond King. If East has it, the slam rolls; if West has it, the slam goes down.

The expert refuses to take that risk. He knows he can force West to lead a Diamond for him. Mr. Expert simply plays a Spade. West wins and is compelled to return a Diamond, conceding declarer a free finesse.

Of course West never would lead a Diamond voluntarily and help declarer, so declarer *forced* him to do so by first stripping away his Hearts and Clubs, then throwing him on lead. West was helpless; he had to play back a Diamond.

It's called an endplay because it usually happens near the end of a hand. Sometimes it's called a "strip-and-endplay" because declarer strips the defenders of the suits they can lead with safety. It is also known as the "throw-in'' because declarer has to have a card to throw West on lead. Here the throw-in card was the Spade Jack.

Is it difficult? It's as easy as falling off a log once you get the hang of it. You have to be able to count to 13, you have to watch carefully all the cards as they fall, and you have to have imagination.

With a One-Way Finesse

In many endplays it's important to force a specific opponent to win the lead. Here's the whole hand so you can watch South engineer his endplay from the beginning. South is in 6 Hearts and West leads the Spade King.

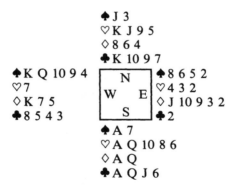

South's count discloses a Spade loser and possibly a Diamond loser. With no way to get rid of the Spade loser, he has to do something about the Diamond. He could finesse, but South foresees a way to eliminate that risk, a way to make West lead Diamonds for him.

Winning the Spade Ace, declarer pulls trumps in three rounds. *This strips trumps from West's hand.*

Taking the A-K-Q-J of Clubs, *he eliminates Clubs from West's hand.* Then the picture is:

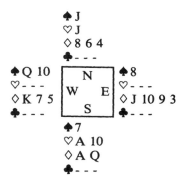

```
                    ♠ J
                    ♡ J
                    ◇ 8 6 4
                    ♣ - - -
    ♠ Q 10    ┌─────────────┐    ♠ 8
    ♡ - - -   │      N      │    ♡ - - -
    ◇ K 7 5   │  W       E  │    ◇ J 10 9 3
    ♣ - - -   │      S      │    ♣ - - -
              └─────────────┘
                    ♠ 7
                    ♡ A 10
                    ◇ A Q
                    ♣ - - -
```

At this auspicious moment, declarer leads a Spade. *This eliminates Spades from the North-South hands,* and simultaneously forces West to win the lead with the Spade Queen. Then, West is endplayed. He has no way out except by giving declarer a trick. If he plays a Spade, declarer ruffs in dummy as he sluffs* the losing Diamond Queen from his hand. If West leads a Diamond, declarer gets a free finesse. Either way the slam is on ice.

Here are the preliminary steps South took to set up the endplay:

- Stripped the opponents of trumps, retaining one or more trumps in both his hand and dummy's.

- Eliminated two side suits from the North-South hands. (Clubs and Spades)

- Threw West on lead to force him to lead the fourth suit or give declarer a ruff and a sluff.

---

* The word "sluff," a synonym for discard, is derived from slough which means to cast off. The word "ruff" is a synonym for trump.

See if you can apply South's technique on this hand:

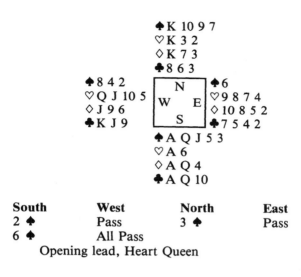

South	West	North	East
2 ♠	Pass	3 ♠	Pass
6 ♠	All Pass		

Opening lead, Heart Queen

South's bookkeeping shows two possible losers in Clubs, but it doesn't worry him a whit because he spots the conditions for an endplay.

What suit does South want an opponent to lead for him? Which opponent? Before reading further, try to plan the execution play-by-play. If you need help, look at all four hands.

Declarer wins the Heart Ace. He pulls trumps in three rounds. *This strips the opponents of trumps so they can't lead that suit.* He cashes the Heart King and ruffs a Heart in his hand. *This eliminates Hearts from the North-South hands so the defenders can't lead that suit without giving declarer a ruff and a sluff.*

Next he runs three rounds of Diamonds, winding up in dummy with the Diamond King. *This eliminates Diamonds from the North-South hands so the defenders can't lead that suit without giving away a trick.* This is the position:

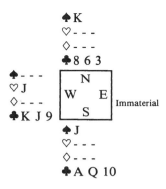

Then declarer comes off dummy with a Club. When East plays low, declarer puts in the 10. West walks out with the Jack and wins the trick.

Then West slumps down in his chair, poor fellow. He squirms and twists, but there is no escape. If he leads a Club, declarer gets a free finesse. If he leads a Heart, declarer trumps in dummy as he throws away the Club Queen.

The A-Q-9 Will Do It

Suppose South hadn't held the Club 10 but had the 9 instead. He still has a sure-to-win position.

```
               ♣8 6 3
♣K J 4    ┌─────────┐   ♣10 7 5
          │   N     │
          │ W   E   │
          │   S     │
          └─────────┘
               ♣A Q 9
```

Leading Clubs from dummy, South covers anything East plays. If East plays low declarer inserts the Club 9, attaining the same result. If East plays the 10 declarer covers with the Queen and forces the King. Now West has to lead from the J-4 into declarer's A-9.

Let's practice on another one. In this hand counting the opening bidder's points led declarer down the right path.

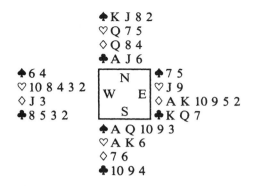

East	South	West	North
1 ◇	1 ♠	Pass	3 ♠
Pass	4 ♠	All Pass	

Opening lead, Diamond Jack

Declarer has four losers in the master hand — two Diamonds and two Clubs. A possible way to eliminate one is to take the double finesse in Clubs, so he asks himself, where are the King-Queen of Clubs? If they're divided he can finesse, losing to East's honor, and finesse again and trap West's honor. The double finesse is a 75% chance.

Checking high-card points declarer finds 26 in his hand and dummy. West's lead of the Diamond Jack accounts for 27 points. All the other points must be in East's hand or he wouldn't have an opening bid! He undoubtedly has both the King and the Queen of Clubs. The double finesse is no longer a 75% chance. It's a 0% chance. Then South realizes he can endplay East and make East lead Clubs!

See if you can strip the hand and skewer East.

South covers the opening Diamond Jack with dummy's Queen. He doesn't expect the Queen to win but he wants to be sure West doesn't have another chance to lead. You'll see why in a minute.

East wins the Diamond King, takes the Diamond Ace, and plays another Diamond. Declarer ruffs with the Spade Ace, a flamboyant card, but he has honors to spare and wants to be certain West can't overruff. On this trick *Diamonds are eliminated from the North-South hands.*

Then declarer extracts trumps in two rounds. Now *trumps are stripped from the opponents' hands.*

Next, declarer cashes dummy's Heart Queen and his Ace and King of Hearts. *This eliminates Hearts from the North-South hands.* The stage is set for the endplay:

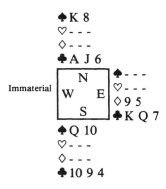

```
              ♠ K 8
              ♡ - - -
              ◊ - - -
              ♣ A J 6
            ┌─────────┐   ♠ - - -
            │    N    │   ♡ - - -
Immaterial  │  W   E  │   ◊ 9 5
            │    S    │   ♣ K Q 7
            └─────────┘
              ♠ Q 10
              ♡ - - -
              ◊ - - -
              ♣ 10 9 4
```

Now the fun begins. From his hand declarer leads the Club 10. West plays low, dummy plays low, and East wins the Queen. East is the victim of an endplay. If he leads a Club it's into dummy's Ace-Jack. If he leads a Diamond declarer throws a Club from his hand and trumps in dummy. Either way declarer wins ten tricks.

It wasn't luck that brought in this game. It was a skillfully executed endplay.

Let's go back to trick one. If the Diamond Jack is not covered by the Queen, East will play the Diamond 2, a signal asking for a switch to another suit. If West shifts to a Club, the endplay is broken up. Declarer has to finesse. When East wins the Queen, he has an exit card. He can lead a Diamond. He is safe because the hand hasn't been stripped.

A Trump for the Throw-in

Sometimes the throw-in card for an endplay is a trump. Here's a hand to illustrate:

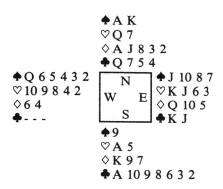

<pre>
                    ♠ A K
                    ♡ Q 7
                    ◇ A J 8 3 2
                    ♣ Q 7 5 4
    ♠ Q 6 5 4 3 2   ♠ J 10 8 7
    ♡ 10 9 8 4 2   ♡ K J 6 3
    ◇ 6 4   ◇ Q 10 5
    ♣ - - -   ♣ K J
                    ♠ 9
                    ♡ A 5
                    ◇ K 9 7
                    ♣ A 10 9 8 6 3 2
</pre>

North	East	South	West
1 ◇	Pass	2 ♣	Pass
4 ♣	Pass	4 NT	Pass
5 ♡	Pass	6 ♣	All Pass

Opening lead, Heart 10

When dummy hits the table declarer is optimistic. It looks like he has one loser, a Diamond, and he might trap that Queen and take all 13 tricks. He puts up dummy's Heart Queen, East covers with the King, and declarer wins the Ace. With only two trumps outstanding declarer plunks down the Club Ace. West can't follow! Unfortunately East now has a sure trump trick and there is still the Diamond problem.

Declarer sets out to force East to lead a Diamond! He takes dummy's Ace-King of Spades, discarding a Heart from his hand. *This eliminates Spades from the North-*

South hands. Leading dummy's last Heart he trumps in his hand. *This eliminates Hearts from the North-South hands.* At this moment the situation is:

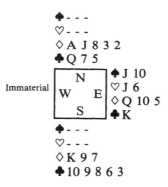

```
              ♠ - - -
              ♡ - - -
              ◇ A J 8 3 2
              ♣ Q 7 5
            ┌─────────┐  ♠ J 10
            │    N    │  ♡ J 6
Immaterial  │ W    E  │  ◇ Q 10 5
            │    S    │  ♣ K
            └─────────┘
              ♠ - - -
              ♡ - - -
              ◇ K 9 7
              ♣ 10 9 8 6 3
```

Now declarer leads a trump, throwing East in the lead with the King. *This strips trumps from East's hand.* East is stuck. If he leads a Diamond declarer gets a free ride. If he leads anything else, declarer discards a Diamond from his hand as he ruffs in dummy. The endplay guarantees the slam.

Flush the Queen

Here's an example where declarer needs to locate a missing Queen to bring in his contract and he has a two-way finesse:

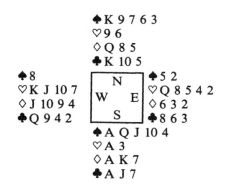

♠ K 9 7 6 3
♡ 9 6
◇ Q 8 5
♣ K 10 5

♠ 8
♡ K J 10 7
◇ J 10 9 4
♣ Q 9 4 2

♠ 5 2
♡ Q 8 5 4 2
◇ 6 3 2
♣ 8 6 3

♠ A Q J 10 4
♡ A 3
◇ A K 7
♣ A J 7

South deals
All vulnerable

South	West	North	East
2 ♠	Pass	3 ♠	Pass
4 NT	Pass	5 ♣	Pass
5 NT	Pass	6 ♡	Pass
6 ♠	All Pass		

Opening lead, Diamond Jack

Declarer has a sure Heart loser and a two-way finesse in Clubs. If his ESP is clicking he can guess who has the dark-haired lady and score his slam; if he guesses wrong the slam goes kaput.

The winning way is to refuse to guess! The winning way is to force an opponent to lead Clubs for you. See if you can manipulate that miracle.

Winning trick one with the Diamond Queen, declarer pulls trumps in two rounds. *It is now impossible for a defender to lead a trump.*

Then he cashes the Ace and King of Diamonds. *This makes it impossible for a defender to lead a Diamond without giving declarer a ruff and a sluff.*

Next he takes his Heart Ace. The situation is:

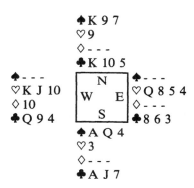

At this precise moment, declarer leads his last Heart. This leaves North and South void, *making it impossible for a defender to lead Hearts without according a ruff-sluff.*

If West wins with the Heart 10, he is endplayed. He has no exit card. If he plays a Club declarer lets it ride to his A-J, winning a free finesse. If he leads a Heart or a Diamond, declarer ruffs in one hand as he sluffs a Club in the other. Either way, with no risk involved, South gets his slam-going trick.

It doesn't help the defense for East to overtake West's 10 with the Queen because East is in the same bind — a Club lead solves declarer's finesse problem, and a Heart lead offers a ruff-sluff. You see why the expert wins so much — when he can pull rabbits like this end play out of his hat.

The Finesse

You can't always set up an endplay because you can't always strip a hand. To help you recognize an endplay let's look at a hand that doesn't have an endplay situation. Give dummy one more Heart. Now, you can't execute an endplay:

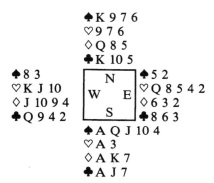

You can't strip this hand because you can't dispose of dummy's other Heart. The opponent who wins the Heart trick can safely return a Heart. You'll trump in your hand but you won't get to sluff a loser from dummy. You're going to have to make the Club guess yourself.

The endplay is an extremely useful tool, but you're still going to have to resort to the finesse lots and lots of times. But don't try a 50% finesse when you have a 100% endplay available.

Make the Opponents Help!

There are many awkward card combinations that cost you a trick if you break the suit, and that cost the opponents a trick if one of them breaks the suit. When you want an adversary to make the first move, check to see if you can endplay him.

(1)   ♣Q 4 3

♣K 10 7 5   N W E S   ♣A 9 8

♣J 6 2

(2)   ♣J 4 3

♣A 9 7   N W E S   ♣Q 10 8 5

♣K 6 2

(3)   ♣K 10 3

♣A 7 6   N W E S   ♣J 8 5 4

♣Q 9 2

In example (1) if South leads Clubs, West will play a little one and it requires North's Queen to force East's Ace. Now West holds the King-10 over the Jack and South can't win a Club trick.

However, if a defender leads the first Club, declarer can always score a trick. If West leads a Club, dummy plays low and East has to play the Ace to prevent declarer's Jack from winning. Then declarer still has the Queen and the Jack. He can force out the King with one honor and win a trick with the other. The same situation exists if East leads a Club.

In example (2) if declarer leads the first Club he'll never get a trick, but if either opponent leads the first Club declarer can always win the King. If East leads, declarer ducks and West has to rise with the Ace to beat the Jack. If West leads, the King is easily a winner.

In example (3) if declarer leads Clubs he might misguess the Jack and win only one trick. If an adversary leads Clubs, declarer is assured of two tricks.

Watch for these situations. When the opponents aren't cooperative in their leads, you might be able to force them to help you. That is what happens on this hand:

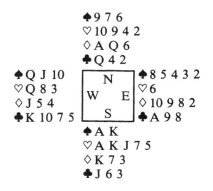

♠9 7 6
♡10 9 4 2
◇A Q 6
♣Q 4 2

♠Q J 10
♡Q 8 3
◇J 5 4
♣K 10 7 5

♠8 5 4 3 2
♡6
◇10 9 8 2
♣A 9 8

♠A K
♡A K J 7 5
◇K 7 3
♣J 6 3

South	West	North	East
1 ♡	Pass	2 ♡	Pass
4 ♡	All Pass		

Opening lead, Spade Queen

Declarer takes the Ace of Spades, then the Ace of Hearts. He crosses to dummy with a Diamond to lead another Heart, thinking he might finesse. When East is unable to follow, declarer runs up with the Heart King. He now has a sure trump loser and three Club losers.

He spots an endplay. Can you execute it?

Collecting the other top Spade, he crosses to dummy with the Diamond Queen and leads a Spade, ruffing in his hand. *This eliminates Spades from the North-South hands.* Then he takes his Diamond King. *This eliminates Diamonds from the North-South hands.* Here's the story:

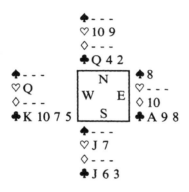

Now declarer presents West with his trump trick and at the same instant endplays West who has no more Spades, no more Hearts, and no more Diamonds. Bared down to Clubs, West has to break the suit. He leads a little Club and East wins the Ace. East happens to have a Diamond in his hand but if he leads a Diamond he gives declarer a ruff-sluff, so East returns a Club. West has to take his King or give dummy the Queen. Thus declarer wins a Club and rolls his contract home.

In No Trump

The endplay can also be a friend in a No Trump contract. However, lacking the advantage of the ruff-sluff available in a suit contract, it is more difficult. You have to be aware of the distribution of each suit all around the table. Here's an illustration:

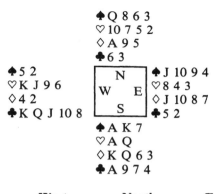

	♠Q 8 6 3	
	♡10 7 5 2	
	◊A 9 5	
	♣6 3	

♠5 2		♠J 10 9 4
♡K J 9 6	N	♡8 4 3
◊4 2	W E	◊J 10 8 7
♣K Q J 10 8	S	♣5 2

	♠A K 7	
	♡A Q	
	◊K Q 6 3	
	♣A 9 7 4	

South	West	North	East
2 NT	Pass	3 ♣	Pass
3 ◊	Pass	3 NT	All Pass

Opening lead, Club King

There are eight tricks off the top — three Spades, three Diamonds, a Heart and a Club — and three chances for the ninth. If either Spades or Diamonds divide evenly, declarer can set up a trick. If both fail, he can fall back on the Heart finesse.

South ducks the first Club and West continues the Queen. Declarer ducks again. West pursues with the Jack. East shows out, revealing West started with five Clubs. South takes the Ace. He plays two top Spades and continues the third round to dummy's Queen. West can't follow, dashing the Spade dream.

Hoping Diamonds behave better, declarer plays the Queen, takes dummy's Ace, and then cashes his King getting another piece of bad news. Again West can't follow.

Now declarer comes up with a sleight-of-hand. *He knows West is out of Spades and out of Diamonds.* Since he can count to 13, *he also knows West holds only two more Clubs.* The other cards have to be Hearts. Here's the actual layout:

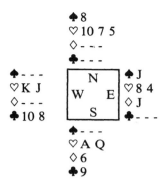

So declarer plays a Club, presenting West with two Club tricks. West is happy to get them, but when he has to lead a Heart from his King-Jack he is miserable. Thus declarer lands his No Trump game with an endplay, and it is the only way the contract can be made.

No defense will beat him if declarer reads the distribution around the table, counts the Club suit, and envisions an endplay.

Defensive Strategy

Watching an endplay is an exhilarating experience when you're the executioner. When the roles are reversed and you're the victim, it's excruciating.

Is there a way to escape from the jaws of this trap? In most cases, no. You are helpless. The endplay is like the Law of Gravity — it works.

Throw Away a Winner!

If you are alert and looking ahead, you can anticipate an endplay, and sometimes you yourself can thwart it. Watch out when declarer starts eliminating from your hand all the cards you can lead without loss to yourself. The blow might be coming. You might be able to parry the thrust by *throwing away a winner*.

As a last resort you can jettison the card that would put you on lead. Refuse to win that traitorous trick. This might cost you a trick, but the endplay is going to cost you a trick for sure. There is always a chance partner has a card that protects the suit.

Here's the cruel thing an opponent did to me in a Women's Pair event. I was playing 4 Hearts after West overcalled a Spade. West led a Club.

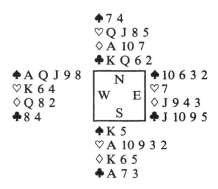

```
                    ♠ 7 4
                    ♡ Q J 8 5
                    ◇ A 10 7
                    ♣ K Q 6 2
   ♠ A Q J 9 8    ┌─────────┐    ♠ 10 6 3 2
   ♡ K 6 4        │    N    │    ♡ 7
   ◇ Q 8 2        │ W     E │    ◇ J 9 4 3
   ♣ 8 4          │    S    │    ♣ J 10 9 5
                  └─────────┘
                    ♠ K 5
                    ♡ A 10 9 3 2
                    ◇ K 6 5
                    ♣ A 7 3
```

There were four losers in my hand — two Spades, one Heart, and one Diamond. Nevertheless, I set out confident I could eliminate one, maybe even two. Winning the opening lead with dummy's Queen, I led the Heart Queen and finessed. Alas, it lost to West's King. She returned another Club and I won the Ace. Now I began to set a trap to endplay West. If she happened to hold the Diamond Queen — as I felt sure she did — I could strip her hand, throw her in with the Queen, and force her to lead a Spade. This would establish my King for the game-going trick!

Pulling the rest of the trumps, I stripped Hearts from her hand. Then I cashed dummy's Club King and ruffed a Club. Now I cashed the Diamond King and led to dummy's Diamond Ace. West saw the endplay coming and threw the Diamond Queen! Winning dummy's Ace, I played another Diamond, hoping West also had the Diamond Jack. It was not to be. East won the Jack and shot a Spade right through by King. Down one! It was a bitter pill to swallow, and I still remember the taste.

If West, who was beautiful Ellasue Chaitt of Gaithersburg, Md., had coddled the Queen, as many other Wests in the event did, she would have been forced to win the third round of Diamonds and would have had to lead a Spade for me.

Another Escape Route

Sometimes when a player sees an endplay coming he can use another ploy. By making a daring discard of the small cards that protect a King or a Queen, he can create a dilemma for declarer, giving the declarer a chance to misjudge the situation. Here's an example:

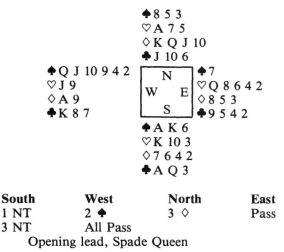

```
              ♠ 8 5 3
              ♡ A 7 5
              ◇ K Q J 10
              ♣ J 10 6
♠ Q J 10 9 4 2   ┌─────────┐   ♠ 7
♡ J 9            │    N    │   ♡ Q 8 6 4 2
◇ A 9            │  W   E  │   ◇ 8 5 3
♣ K 8 7          │    S    │   ♣ 9 5 4 2
                 └─────────┘
              ♠ A K 6
              ♡ K 10 3
              ◇ 7 6 4 2
              ♣ A Q 3
```

South	West	North	East
1 NT	2 ♠	3 ◇	Pass
3 NT	All Pass		

Opening lead, Spade Queen

South wins the Spade King and leads a Diamond. West takes the Ace and plays the Spade Jack. Declarer wins the Ace.

When declarer next cashes three Diamonds West has to find two pitches and throws a little Club and a little Spade.

Harkening back to West's overcall, South decides it's useless to finesse East for the Club King. There are 27 points in the North-South hands and West is likely to hold the rest. Declarer decides to endplay West for a Club lead.

Declarer cashes the Ace and King of Hearts and throws West on lead with a Spade. West collects three Spade tricks and is book-in but has to lead a Club into the Ace-Queen.

Is there any way West can avoid the throw-in? Yes, if he has the nerve. Not many players do. He can avoid the trap by smoothly throwing two Clubs on the Diamonds, blanking down to the singleton King! Declarer is almost sure to misread the situation. Whether he tries the finesse or the endplay, West's strategy pays off. If declarer tries the endplay, West has enough Spades left to beat the contract. If declarer tries the Club finesse, West wins ALL the rest of the tricks.

There is the threat declarer will bang down the Club Ace, smothering the King, and win his Queen and his Jack for ten tricks. West takes the gamble because it's the only way to set the contract. The chance to beat the contract is easily worth the risk of an overtrick.

Partner to the Rescue

Occasionally your partner can rescue you by straining to gain the lead, heroically trumping your trick or overtaking your trick, winning unnecessarily to take you off an endplay. Here's a sample:

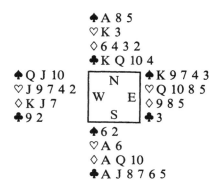

```
              ♠ A 8 5
              ♡ K 3
              ◊ 6 4 3 2
              ♣ K Q 10 4
  ♠ Q J 10         N        ♠ K 9 7 4 3
  ♡ J 9 7 4 2   W     E     ♡ Q 10 8 5
  ◊ K J 7                   ◊ 9 8 5
  ♣ 9 2            S        ♣ 3
              ♠ 6 2
              ♡ A 6
              ◊ A Q 10
              ♣ A J 8 7 6 5
```

South	West	North	East
1 ♣	Pass	3 ♣	Pass
5 ♣	All Pass		

Opening lead, Spade Queen

Declarer ducks the opening lead of the Spade Queen and East stops to wonder why. Seeing all those little Diamonds in dummy, he suspects partner is going to be subjected to an endplay. East overtakes partner's Spade Queen with the King and at trick two plays a Diamond through declarer. This averts the endplay because West wins a Diamond trick at a time when he has a safe exit card.

If East allows West to win trick one, the contract is unbeatable. Next declarer wins the Spade Ace, pulls trumps, ruffs a Spade to eliminate that suit, and takes the Ace and King of Hearts to eliminate that suit. Now the stage is set. He leads a Diamond from dummy, inserting the 10. When West wins he has no safe return and has to give declarer a trick. A Heart offers a ruff and a sluff while a Diamond yields a free finesse.

Drill on Endplays

(1) Against West's 6 Hearts, North leads the Club King.

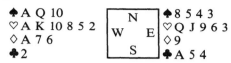

♠ A Q 10
♡ A K 10 8 5 2
◇ A 7 6
♣ 2

♠ 8 5 4 3
♡ Q J 9 6 3
◇ 9
♣ A 5 4

Trumps are divided. North has three Spades to the King-Jack. Can you guarantee the contract?

(2) Against West's 5 Diamonds, North leads the Spade King.

♠ A 7 2
♡ A J 3
◇ A K 8 6 4 2
♣ 8

♠ 8 6 5
♡ K 10 4
◇ Q J 10 7
♣ A J 10

Trumps are divided 2-1. Can you plan the play so you're sure of 11 tricks?

(3) Against South's 6 No Trump, West leads the Club Jack.

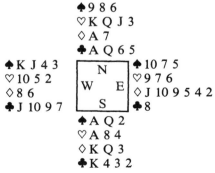

♠ 9 8 6
♡ K Q J 3
◇ A 7
♣ A Q 6 5

♠ K J 4 3
♡ 10 5 2
◇ 8 6
♣ J 10 9 7

♠ 10 7 5
♡ 9 7 6
◇ J 10 9 5 4 2
♣ 8

♠ A Q 2
♡ A 8 4
◇ K Q 3
♣ K 4 3 2

How many ready-made tricks does South have?
What are the options for one more trick?
How would you play it?
Is there any way West can save himself from your strategy?

25. With the Touch of a Master

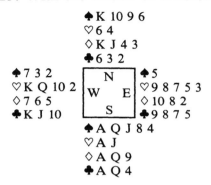

```
              ♠ K 10 9 6
              ♡ 6 4
              ◇ K J 4 3
              ♣ 6 3 2
♠ 7 3 2                        ♠ 5
♡ K Q 10 2      N             ♡ 9 8 7 5 3
◇ 7 6 5      W     E          ◇ 10 8 2
♣ K J 10        S             ♣ 9 8 7 5
              ♠ A Q J 8 4
              ♡ A J
              ◇ A Q 9
              ♣ A Q 4
```

North deals
East-West vulnerable

North	East	South	West
Pass	Pass	2 ♠	Pass
3 ♠	Pass	6 ♠	All Pass

Opening lead, Heart King

Viewing dummy with a steady eye, South spotted three possible losers — two Clubs and a Heart. He could throw one loser on dummy's extra Diamond winner and he could afford to surrender one loser and still slide in with his slam.

What could he do about the third loser? Finesse East for the Club King? Exploring a little further, studying a little more, declarer suddenly saw a light at the end of the tunnel that illuminated a 100% play for his contract. Can you find it?

His plan was to endplay West and force West to lead a Club for him! This was the way he manipulated this feat. Winning trick one with the Heart Ace, he drew trumps. It took three rounds. *This eliminated Spades from West's hand.*

Then declarer played the Diamond Ace-Queen-King-Jack, in that order. (On the last Diamond he dropped a

Club loser from his hand.) Now *Diamonds were eliminated from West's hand.* This was the situation:

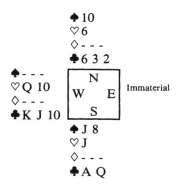

```
              ♠ 10
              ♡ 6
              ◇ - - -
              ♣ 6 3 2
  ♠ - - -      ┌─────────┐
  ♡ Q 10       │    N    │   Immaterial
  ◇ - - -      │ W     E │
  ♣ K J 10     │    S    │
              └─────────┘
              ♠ J 8
              ♡ J
              ◇ - - -
              ♣ A Q
```

Next, declarer smartly led a Heart and presented West with his Queen, simultaneously *eliminating the Heart suit from the North-South hands.*

When West captured this trick he was a dead duck. He was endplayed. If he returned a Heart declarer could trump in dummy as he discarded the Club Queen from his hand. If he returned a Club, he had to lead away from his King. It was frustrating.

Finally, with a tremor in his fingers, West laid down the Club Jack, making a silent prayer his partner held the Queen. It was not to be. His prayer went unanswered. South brought forth the Queen and pulled in the rest of the tricks for a well-earned slam.

26. Let the Finesser Beware!

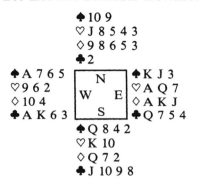

```
              ♠ 10 9
              ♡ J 8 5 4 3
              ◇ 9 8 6 5 3
              ♣ 2
♠ A 7 6 5                    ♠ K J 3
♡ 9 6 2         N           ♡ A Q 7
◇ 10 4      W       E       ◇ A K J
♣ A K 6 3       S           ♣ Q 7 5 4
              ♠ Q 8 4 2
              ♡ K 10
              ◇ Q 7 2
              ♣ J 10 9 8
```

East deals
All vulnerable

East	South	West	North
1 ♣	Pass	1 ♠	Pass
3 NT	All Pass		

Opening lead, Club Jack

South led the Club Jack and declarer won it in dummy with the King. Declarer's survey showed eight easy tricks — three Clubs, two Spades, one Heart, and two Diamonds. Clubs might contribute one more to bring in the game.

Then visions of overtricks danced in his head. He could take a finesse for the Spade Queen, a finesse for the Heart King, and a finesse for the Diamond Queen. If those cards happened to be placed favorably he might take a dozen tricks.

East decided first to investigate the Club distribution. He played a second round of the suit to his Queen. North showed out. By counting Clubs and imagining what other cards South held in his hand, declarer decided to endplay South. He took his third Club winner and then played a fourth round. South, of course, won.

With no more Clubs in his hand, South had to lead a Spade, a Heart, or a Diamond. Any one would give declarer a free finesse.

Oh, how sweet it was!

South selected a Spade. Declarer let it ride around to his King-Jack and the Jack won. This assured the nine-trick game, but there is more to tell.

East cashed the Spade King and the Ace. When the suit failed to break, East simply played dummy's last Spade and presented South with another trick, the Spade Queen.

Again South was endplayed. He held only red cards and he had to play one of them. He pulled out a Diamond. Declarer won the Jack and took the Ace-King. The Heart Ace was trick ten, so East pirouetted in with an overtrick.

It happened at a duplicate game and the board moved to the next table where East #2 reached the same contract and received the same lead. East #2 had never learned the endplay but he was a fearless finesser. He won dummy's Club King and plunged into the Spade finessee. It lost to South who returned a second Club. Declarer took this in his hand, slightly startled when North was unable to follow suit.

Proceeding with his Spade work, East #2 cashed the King and crossed to dummy's Ace. Of course the suit didn't split, but East refused to brood. Realizing North started with a fistful of red cards, he decided the Diamond and Heart finesses were odds-on favorites.

With renewed confidence he led a Diamond and inserted the Jack. South walked out with the Queen and hastened to collect his ranking Spade. Then South shot back the Club 9.

Dummy's Ace won. Since this was his last trip to the board, declarer led a Heart and bet with the Queen. South won the King and led Clubs again. This time his was the big one so that made five tricks for North-South — two Spades, one Heart, one Diamond, and one Club. The rest belonged to a sobered East. Down one.

27. How To Cook a Goose

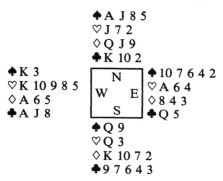

```
              ♠ A J 8 5
              ♡ J 7 2
              ◇ Q J 9
              ♣ K 10 2
♠ K 3                          ♠ 10 7 6 4 2
♡ K 10 9 8 5     N             ♡ A 6 4
◇ A 6 5        W   E           ◇ 8 4 3
♣ A J 8          S             ♣ Q 5
              ♠ Q 9
              ♡ Q 3
              ◇ K 10 7 2
              ♣ 9 7 6 4 3
```

South deals
None vulnerable

South	West	North	East
Pass	1 ♡	Double	2 ♡
All Pass			

Opening lead, Diamond Queen

After West opened the bidding with a Heart, North made a takeout double. If East had passed, South would have called 2 Clubs and that contract was a sure thing, but East euchred out a Heart raise and the auction died.

Declarer's quick reconnaissance revealed six losers — two Spades, one Heart, two Diamonds, and one Club. On the bidding it was obvious North had the Club King so the Club finesse was doomed. North undoubtedly held the Spade Ace so it was pointless to lead toward the King. It all spelled down one.

But West refused to surrender and set out to try to force North to break the Spade suit. Since North was as eager to set the contract as West was to bring it in, the only way to accomplish this was to make it impossible for North to play anything else. He had to be endplayed.

Meanwhile South, who couldn't even eke out a bid, became the dangerous opponent. He must be kept out of the lead, for surely South would find the devilish switch of a Spade through declarer's King.

For this reason, when North opened the Diamond Queen and South encouraged with the 7, declarer ducked. Obviously South had the King and declarer couldn't afford to let South gain the lead with it.

North played the Diamond Jack, South completed his echo by dropping the deuce, and again, declarer held back the Ace. North continued with the Diamond 9, South covered with the 10, and declarer took the Ace. *This eliminated Diamonds from North's hand.*

Declarer played the Ace and the King of trumps, then another trump. North won the Jack. *This eliminated Hearts from North's hand* and he was on lead again.

Holding only black cards, North was endplayed. He led the Club 2. Dummy's Queen captured the trick, a pleasant gift. Nevertheless, declarer still faced the same six losers. He cashed the Club Ace and played the Club Jack. West, bared down to the King, was forced to win.

The telling moment had arrived. West's careful conniving had backed North into a corner. Again he was endplayed. With only Spades in his hand he was in the unhappy position of having to lead the suit. He laid down the Ace, then a low Spade, and declarer's King won. West had his contract.

South could have been a hero but he went to sleep on his feet, or whatever he was on. He, too, heard the bidding and it should have pointed him in the right direction. Partner needed a Spade lead through declarer and South should have made a Herculean effort to gain the lead. He should have jumped on the Diamond Jack with the King. Now, no matter how declarer struggled, South would win the King or the 10 and, whichever and whenever, could lower the boom by laying down the Spade Queen. This would cook West's goose.

28. Smoking Out a Queen

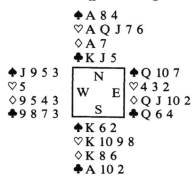

```
              ♠ A 8 4
              ♡ A Q J 7 6
              ◇ A 7
              ♣ K J 5
  ♠ J 9 5 3    ┌─────┐    ♠ Q 10 7
  ♡ 5          │  N  │    ♡ 4 3 2
  ◇ 9 5 4 3    │W   E│    ◇ Q J 10 2
  ♣ 9 8 7 3    │  S  │    ♣ Q 6 4
              └─────┘
              ♠ K 6 2
              ♡ K 10 9 8
              ◇ K 8 6
              ♣ A 10 2
```

West deals
North-South vulnerable

West	North	East	South
Pass	1 ♡	Pass	3 ♡
Pass	4 NT	Pass	5 ◇
Pass	6 ♡	All Pass	

Opening lead, Diamond Queen

South's jump raise propelled North into dreams of a slam. When his request for Aces revealed the partnership had all four, he bid 6 Hearts.

East led the Diamond Queen and declarer stopped to analyze his assets. He saw a Spade loser and a possible Club loser. In a few seconds he saw a strategy that would guarantee his slam.

He won the Diamond Ace and pulled trumps in three rounds. *This eliminated Hearts from the opponents' hands.*

Then he won the Diamond King and ruffed a Diamond. *This eliminated Diamonds from the North-South hands.*

Next, he cashed the Ace-King of Spades. With an air of confidence, North reared back in his chair. The cards remaining in everybody's hands were:

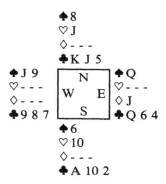

At this moment he briskly continued a third Spade. On this trick *Spades were eliminated from the North-South hands.* Whoever won this trick, East or West, would be the victim of an endplay.

East took the trick and was stymied. If he led a Diamond declarer would ruff in one hand and sluff a Club loser in the other. If he led a Club declarer had a free finesse. Seeing the hopelessness of a Diamond, East played back a Club. Dummy followed low, West low, and declarer won the Jack and claimed the slam.

Even if East had seen the endplay coming and jettisoned the Spade Queen, it wouldn't have helped. If West had won the trick, declarer would have been in the same comfortable position. A Spade return would give declarer a ruff-sluff, or if West led a Club, declarer would let it ride to dummy's Ace-10.

Thus North found a cast-iron play for his contract without risking a guess for the Club Queen — and also got a story to tell — good for at least a week.

VIII. SQUEEZES ARE FUN

When you need one more trick and you see no possibility whatsoever, don't give up. Take all your winners and watch what happens. You might get a gift from Heaven . . . or from your opponents.

A multitude of contracts have been fulfilled this way. You've seen it happen. Declarer runs a string of tricks, a defender misguesses and discards wrong, and some inconsequential little card is established. At the end everybody laughs, declarer loudest of all.

The chances are that defender didn't misguess. The chances are the discard was literally squeezed out of him. He was burdened with the protection of two suits and didn't have a card to spare. Whatever he did, he gave away a trick. That's the essence of the squeeze.

People shy away from studying this card play saying it's too complex. Some squeezes are so easy Mr. Stumblebum could fall into the right play without realizing what he's doing. Watch him here:

```
                    ♠ 10 9 8
                    ♡ K 7 2
                    ◇ 7 6 3
                    ♣ A K Q 2
        ♠ 3                        ♠ 5 4 2
        ♡ J 10 9 8    ┌─────┐      ♡ A Q 6 5 4 3
        ◇ J 10 9 8    │  N  │      ◇ 5 4
        ♣ J 10 9 8    │W   E│      ♣ 4 3
                      │  S  │
                      └─────┘
                    ♠ A K Q J 7 6
                    ♡ - - -
                    ◇ A K Q 2
                    ♣ 7 6 5
```

South	West	North	East
2 ♠	Pass	3 ♠	Pass
4 ◇	Pass	5 Clubs	Pass
5 ◇	Pass	6 ♣	Pass
7 ♠	All Pass		

Opening lead, Heart Jack

Just a word about the bidding. This isn't the way Mr. Stumblebum's auction went; it's better not to make a record of that! It is the way some other folks would bid it. Since South had a void, he didn't want to use the Blackwood Convention to ask North how many Aces he had. If partner had just one Ace — as was the actual case — South needed to know *which* Ace.

Consequently, after the trump suit was agreed on, South cue-bid 4 Diamonds to show his lowest ranking Ace, and North cue-bid 5 Clubs to show his lowest ranking Ace. When South rebid Diamonds, he showed the King. When North rebid Clubs, he showed that King. Then South leaped all the way.

Back to Mr. Stumblebum. When he examined dummy, he found one loser and twelve instant winners — six Spades, three Diamonds, and three Clubs. Searching for one more winner he surfaced with these ideas:

Idea 1: If the six outstanding Clubs split 3-3, dummy's deuce will bring in the Grand Slam.

Idea 2: If the six outstanding Diamonds split 3-3, the Diamond deuce will rescue the contract. Since the odds are that both suits will divide 4-2, is there any other hope? If trumps break 2-2, dummy can ruff the Diamond deuce. Then Mr. Stumblebum had an inspiration.

Idea 3: If he played Diamonds and Club last, maybe the opponents would get mixed up and discard wrong!

On the opening lead of the Heart Jack, declarer tried dummy's King, but East topped it with the Ace, so Mr. Stumblebum ruffed. Next, he ran his string of Spades. West followed to the first round, then threw away all of his Hearts. Here was the setup with one trump to go:

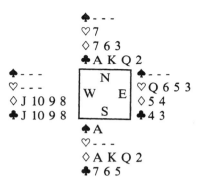

When Mr. Stumblebum played his *last* Spade, West was squeezed. He couldn't afford a discard, yet he had to play to the trick. He writhed and wiggled and finally let go of a Diamond.

That card was very interesting to Mr. Stumblebum, who now cashed the Ace-King-Queen of Diamonds and counted the Diamonds as they fell. When all were accounted for, the Diamond deuce was established and Mr. Stumblebum had his critical thirteenth trick as well as his first Grand Slam.

Did West make a mistake? No. If West had discarded a Club the story would have the same happy ending. Then Mr. Stumblebum would have to try Clubs. When the last outstanding Club fell, again the slam would come home.

Many players, trying to coax a crucial discard from the opponents, cash all their trumps except the last one. They clutch it tight to their chests, thinking they need it to protect themselves. That's a mistake. It's the last trump (or winner) that forces the fatal discard. It's the squeeze card.

This squeeze was easy. In real life this grand slam would be made by most players. It requires no special technique as long as declarer plays *all* of his trumps. Mr. Stumblebum didn't even have to do much counting. He just watched for a Club or a Diamond. When a Diamond appeared he kept track of that one suit. After the Diamond suit was tested, if that deuce wasn't established, all he could do was try Clubs.

Let's look at what happened because the requisites for a squeeze were revealed:

1. Declarer had only one loser.
2. Declarer had two cards in two different suits threatening to become winners. These are called "threat cards."
3. One defender was busy protecting both suits, while the other defender was helpless.
4. There was an entry to each threat card.

1. Correct the Count

A squeeze yields one trick and one trick only. Therefore, to execute a squeeze declarer must have one loser and one loser only. Imagine for a moment Mr. Stumblebum was a Queen lighter and only bid 6 Spades. He begins with two losers. If he's planning to develop a squeeze he must surrender one loser as soon as possible.

If South is in 4 Spades and hopes to make it on a squeeze, he must first surrender three tricks. Only then will the squeeze mechanism function. In a 3 No Trump contract when declarer has eight winners and hopes a squeeze will yield the ninth, he must first get rid of the four surplus losers.

If the defenders don't cash their winners, declarer must force them to take them. The crux of the matter is: when declarer lays down the squeeze card, every card in his hand must be a winner except one. That's why we gave Mr. Stumblebum a grand slam. The count was right from the start.

The mechanism is the same one you use every morning before brushing your teeth. You squeeze the toothpaste tube on each side to force the paste out. The toothpaste has to do what you want it to do when you make the space on the inside tight. Likewise, when you tighten your bridge hand by cutting down to one loser, you put pressure on an opponent, who is busy protecting two suits, to emit a vital card.

2. Two Threat Cards

In the grand slam hand, Mr. Stumblebum had two threat cards in two different suits, the Diamond 2 and the Club 2. Since the threat cards were in separate hands, Mr. Stumblebum wasn't squeezed. However, West had to protect both suits all by himself, so he got squeezed.

Whenever declarer's threat cards are in opposite hands a squeeze operates just as effectively against either opponent. Swap the East and West hands and Mr. Stumblebum won't mind. He can squeeze East just as easily.

3. One Defender Busy in Two Suits

A bridge hand contains idle cards that are worthless and busy cards that are useful as potential winners or as guards of potential winners. In that grand slam, West had five idle cards — one Spade and four Hearts. He had eight busy cards — four Diamonds and four Clubs. After he used up all his idle cards on the first five tricks, he was forced to discard a busy card on the sixth trick.

If East had been able to protect one of these suits the burden would have been divided and there would have been no squeeze. Each defender would have had plenty of idle cards and could have held onto all his busy cards.

4. Entries

Of course you have to have an entry. A card isn't much of a threat if you can't get to it. Here entries aren't a problem. But if Mr. Stumblebum cashes three Clubs too soon, he destroys his entry to dummy, so the Club deuce isn't a threat and the squeeze fails.

When the squeeze card is played there must be an entry to the opposite hand.

Only One Loser

Let's take away Mr. Stumblebum's Diamond Queen and make it 6 Spades to check out the fundamental premise, *declarer must be within one trick of his contract.*

If you feel like trying your squeeze skill before reading on, go ahead and have fun. West still kicks off with the Heart Jack.

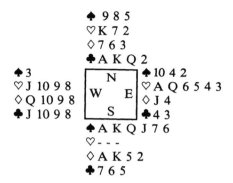

```
            ♠ 9 8 5
            ♡ K 7 2
            ◇ 7 6 3
            ♣ A K Q 2
♠ 3                         ♠ 10 4 2
♡ J 10 9 8      N           ♡ A Q 6 5 4 3
◇ Q 10 9 8   W   E          ◇ J 4
♣ J 10 9 8      S           ♣ 4 3
            ♠ A K Q J 7 6
            ♡ - - -
            ◇ A K 5 2
            ♣ 7 6 5
```

When dummy came down, South found eleven sure winners and two Diamond losers. He had no resources unless the minor suits broke, so naturally, he looked for a squeeze.

The play started exactly the same, declarer covering the Heart Jack with the King, East putting up the Ace, and declarer ruffing. Now watch West's hand and notice what happens if declarer immediately runs all his trumps. Just before the last trump the situation is:

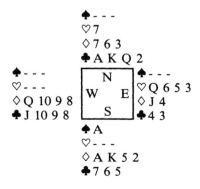

```
            ♠ - - -
            ♡ 7
            ◇ 7 6 3
            ♣ A K Q 2
♠ - - -                     ♠ - - -
♡ - - -         N           ♡ Q 6 5 3
◇ Q 10 9 8   W   E          ◇ J 4
♣ J 10 9 8      S           ♣ 4 3
            ♠ A
            ♡ - - -
            ◇ A K 5 2
            ♣ 7 6 5
```

When declarer lays down his Spade Ace, West suffers no anguish. He can throw a Diamond. He's still going to win the third round of Diamonds and a Club and blow South's slam to smithereens. He isn't squeezed because declarer failed to cut his losers down to one. The superfluous card got in the way.

Back up. Begin again. This time after South ruffs the opening Heart and pulls trumps, he then *surrenders a Diamond*. This corrects the count; declarer has only one loser left. Now, a miracle takes place.

Declarer wins any return and it doesn't matter what it is. Say it's a Diamond. He takes the King and then runs every trump. Before the last one, the position is:

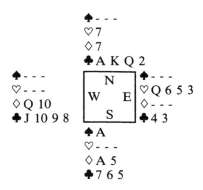

```
                    ♠ - - -
                    ♡ 7
                    ◇ 7
                    ♣ A K Q 2
        ♠ - - -      ┌─────────┐      ♠ - - -
        ♡ - - -      │    N    │      ♡ Q 6 5 3
        ◇ Q 10       │ W     E │      ◇ - - -
        ♣ J 10 9 8   │    S    │      ♣ 4 3
                     └─────────┘
                    ♠ A
                    ♡ - - -
                    ◇ A 5
                    ♣ 7 6 5
```

Now when declarer cashes his last Spade, West is truly and effectively squeezed. There is no escape. All his cards are busy. If West throws the Diamond 10, declarer's little Diamond becomes a winner. If West chooses instead to discard a Club, dummy's Club deuce becomes good. Either way South wins the rest of the tricks and romps in with his slam.

Declarer's Threat Cards

In both example hands declarer's threat cards were in separate hands. You can also execute a squeeze with both threat cards in the same hand providing the defender protecting the two suits has to discard *before* the hand with the two threat cards.

Let's check that out in a No Trump contract:

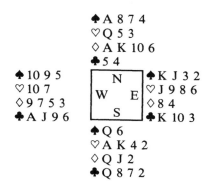

```
                    ♠ A 8 7 4
                    ♡ Q 5 3
                    ◇ A K 10 6
                    ♣ 5 4
  ♠ 10 9 5        ┌─────────┐        ♠ K J 3 2
  ♡ 10 7          │    N    │        ♡ J 9 8 6
  ◇ 9 7 5 3       │ W     E │        ◇ 8 4
  ♣ A J 9 6       │    S    │        ♣ K 10 3
                  └─────────┘
                    ♠ Q 6
                    ♡ A K 4 2
                    ◇ Q J 2
                    ♣ Q 8 7 2
```

South	West	North	East
1 ♣	Pass	1 ◇	Pass
1 ♡	Pass	1 ♠	Pass
1 NT	Pass	3 NT	All Pass

Opening lead, Club 6

West struck oil when he led the Club 6. East won the King, returned the 10, and the defense gobbled up the first four tricks. On the last Club East signaled violently with the Spade Jack. Complying with partner's request, West switched to a Spade, laying down the 10.

Declarer paused to reassess. At this moment he had eight winners ready-to-go and one loser. The opponents had done one favor for him. They had corrected the count so he had the first requirement for a squeeze.

Idea 1: If Hearts were 3-3, he could establish the fourth Heart in his hand.

Idea 2: If the defenders were fooling and West had the Spade King, he could let this trick ride to his Queen. He vetoed that idea. He believed East held the King.

Idea 3: If East held the Spade King and also four Hearts, he would be busy in two suits. Nothing to do but run the Diamonds!

Declarer rose with the Spade Ace and took three Diamonds. As he was about to lead the last Diamond, the picture was:

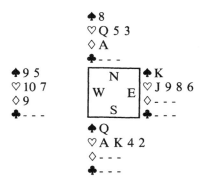

```
              ♠ 8
              ♡ Q 5 3
              ◇ A
              ♣ - - -
   ♠ 9 5                    ♠ K
   ♡ 10 7      N            ♡ J 9 8 6
   ◇ 9      W     E         ◇ - - -
   ♣ - - -      S           ♣ - - -
              ♠ Q
              ♡ A K 4 2
              ◇ - - -
              ♣ - - -
```

Now dummy's Diamond Ace turned on the heat. Every card in East's hand was busy. Every card in South's hand was busy, too, but East had to discard *before* South. Thus declarer could adjust his own discard to whatever East chose. If East held onto the Spade King, he had to let go of a Heart. If he hung onto four Hearts, he had to let go of the Spade King.

East didn't have a chance because his hand was tight. His setting trick was squeezed right out of the toothpaste tube. Since he didn't feel he could throw the Spade King, he threw a Heart. Then declarer discarded the Spade Queen and the neat little Heart 4 brought in the game.

There is a famous player and bridge theorist, Alvin Roth of New York City, who boasts he never lets his partner get squeezed. If Roth had been West, after winning the second Club trick, with malice aforethought he would have switched to a Spade. Look what happens! South has not reached the all-but-one position necessary for a squeeze and he can't get that ninth trick.

If South goes up with the Spade Ace he can take his original eight winners and that's all. East has an idle card and isn't squeezed. If he doesn't go up with the Ace, East wins the King, returns another Club, and the defenders take the first five tricks.

One Defender Busy in Two Suits

Squeezes are easier in a suit contract because declarer's ability to ruff gives him added dexterity. Sometimes both defenders hold controls over one threat card, but declarer can ruff a round or two and transfer the full burden to one opponent.

The following hand illustrates the technique:

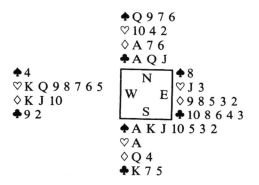

```
                    ♠ Q 9 7 6
                    ♡ 10 4 2
                    ◇ A 7 6
                    ♣ A Q J
    ♠ 4                         ♠ 8
    ♡ K Q 9 8 7 6 5    N        ♡ J 3
    ◇ K J 10         W   E      ◇ 9 8 5 3 2
    ♣ 9 2              S        ♣ 10 8 6 4 3
                    ♠ A K J 10 5 3 2
                    ♡ A
                    ◇ Q 4
                    ♣ K 7 5
```

South	West	North	East
1 ♠	4 ♡	4 ♠	Pass
4 NT	Pass	5 ♡	Pass
6 ♠	All Pass		

Opening lead, Heart King

When declarer studied his assets he saw 12 tricks, but he was playing in a tournament where an overtrick can be worth its weight in uranium. The challenge was to take every one.

He found the conditions for a squeeze: (1) He had one loser. (2) He had two threat cards, the Diamond Queen in his hand and the Heart 10 in dummy. (3) He quite reasonably decided West, for his big bid, had the Diamond King. The opening lead revealed West also had the Heart Queen, so West was busy in two suits. (4) The Diamond Ace was an entry to dummy's threat card.

He won the Heart Ace, pulled trumps, and took all three Clubs, winding up in dummy. Next he made a key play. (You'll see why later.) He led a little Heart, East played the Jack, and declarer ruffed in his hand.

Then he ran all his trumps, baring down to this three-card position:

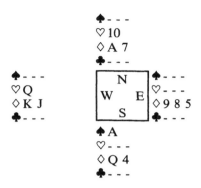

When South played the last Spade poor West was pulverized. If he released a Diamond, he had to unguard the Diamond King; if he released a Heart, he set up dummy's 10. Actually, he let go of the Diamond Jack, so dummy threw the Heart 10. Then South led a low Diamond to the Ace, impaling West's King, and a Diamond back to his Queen for the all-important thirteenth trick.

Why was the Heart ruff important? Couldn't declarer just run Spades and still squeeze West down to the same position? He could, but East would be able to hold onto the Heart Jack and if West read the situation correctly, West could throw away the Heart Queen and hold both Diamonds. By trumping out East's Jack of Hearts declarer transferred to West the full responsibility for Hearts.

Squeeze Vocabulary

This technique has a fancy name. You don't have to learn it, but you might have fun bandying it about. It's called "isolating the menace."

There's another technical term. Cutting your losers down to one is called "rectifying the count." You don't have to know that, either, to operate a squeeze, but it does have a nice ring.

You might have fun someday telling your spouse, "After you rectified the count, sweetheart, you forgot to isolate the menace!"

The Entry

When setting the stage for a squeeze, plan ahead what card will be the entry to the opposite hand. Usually one hand is strong and has lots of entries. The other hand is often weak and has few. Once you find your entry to the weak hand, that fact guides you to the correct sequence for running your string of tricks. Here's an illustration:

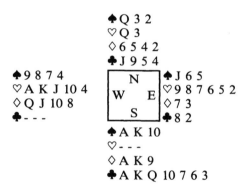

South	West	North	East
2 ♣	2 ♡	Pass	4 ♡
5 ♣	5 ♡	6 ♣	Pass
7 ♣	All Pass		

Opening lead, Heart King

As soon as declarer got a glimpse of dummy, he clocked off 12 tricks, but he didn't have any possible place to put his Diamond loser and appeared destined to go down one. This alerted him to look for a squeeze.

West's opening lead of the King of Hearts indicated he also held the Ace, so dummy's Queen of Hearts was a threat card against West. If West also had to protect Diamonds, declarer's own Diamond 9 would be the other threat card.

South started by ruffing the opening lead, then ran five trumps producing this situation:

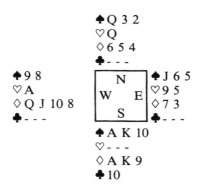

When declarer led his last Club, West discarded a Diamond and so did dummy. Then declarer cashed the Ace-King of Spades and still West felt no pinch because he could follow suit. The story was:

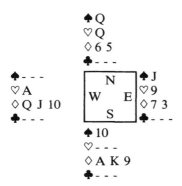

When declarer led the Spade 10, West was caught in a pincer movement. He couldn't afford to discard the Heart Ace and make dummy's Queen a winner, nor could he part with a Diamond. He was hopelessly squeezed and had to give up an important card. He finally let go of a Diamond. Then declarer came off dummy with a Diamond to his Ace-King, and the Diamond 9 brought in the grand slam.

When declarer realized the Spade Queen had to be held in reserve as an entry to dummy, he saw he had to run the trump winners before the Spade winners.

Squeeze Drill

(1) North leads the Club King against 7 No Trump by West.

♠ Q 4   ♠ A K 6 5
♡ A K J 10   ♡ Q 7 2
◊ A K 5 4   ◊ Q J 7
♣ A J 10   ♣ 6 4 2

How many tricks does West have? What chance does he have of making one more?

(2) North leads the Club Queen against West's 3 No Trump contract and the defenders take the first four tricks, then switch to a Heart.

♠ A K 5   ♠ J 9 7 4
♡ K 6 4   ♡ A Q 7
◊ A K 7 2   ◊ Q 8 6
♣ 9 5 3   ♣ 7 4 2

Can declarer make the hand if North holds Q-x-x of Spades and four Diamonds? On the fourth Club, what does declarer discard from his hand? from dummy?

(3) After North opens the bidding with a Heart, West winds up playing 5 Clubs. North leads the Spade King and then switches to the Heart Queen.

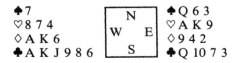

♠ 7   ♠ Q 6 3
♡ 8 7 4   ♡ A K 9
◊ A K 6   ◊ 9 4 2
♣ A K J 9 8 6 ♣ Q 10 7 3

How many tricks does declarer have? What are his chances of making his contract?

29. Keep the Faith: Correct the Count!

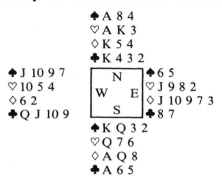

```
              ♠ A 8 4
              ♡ A K 3
              ◇ K 5 4
              ♣ K 4 3 2
♠ J 10 9 7                    ♠ 6 5
♡ 10 5 4          N          ♡ J 9 8 2
◇ 6 2         W       E      ◇ J 10 9 7 3
♣ Q J 10 9        S          ♣ 8 7
              ♠ K Q 3 2
              ♡ Q 7 6
              ◇ A Q 8
              ♣ A 6 5
```

North deals
All vulnerable

North	East	South	West
1 NT	Pass	6 NT	All Pass

Opening lead, Diamond Jack

Facing 11 sure-fire winners — three Spades, three Hearts, three Diamonds, and two Clubs — North cast around for a way to turn one more trick. He might he able to set up a long Spade in dummy or establish the long Club in his own hand.

If neither suit broke well, there was another chance. If the same defender had to protect Spades and Clubs, that defender could be squeezed. He checked out the squeeze situation:

1. Since he had two losers, he must correct the count and get rid of the surplus trick. He would give up a Club, which would be a move also toward setting up that suit.

2. He had two threat cards — dummy's long Spade and his own long Club.

3. If one opponent had to protect both black suits, he could be squeezed.

4. The entry to each hand would be a Spade, so Spades would be played last.

North won the first trick with dummy's Diamond Queen. Then he led dummy's Club 5. West played the 9 and declarer kept the faith ... he ... ducked the trick. West won and played another Club. Declarer took dummy's Ace.

Now he ran all his red winners. On the Ace-King-Queen of Hearts, West followed nonchalantly. On the King of Diamonds, West continued to discard easily and in rhythm. This was the round-up with one more Diamond to go:

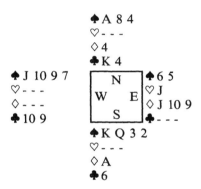

When dummy's Diamond Ace came down, West crumbled. He needed every card he had as guards. He crossed his knees, swung his foot, and looked at the ceiling. But the ceiling couldn't help.

Feeling he must hold onto Spades, he pitched a Club. Declarer led a Club to his King and cashed the Club 4, now the last Club in the deck.

The Ace-King-Queen of Spades made a dozen tricks and it was all over except the applause.

30. The Powerful Weapon

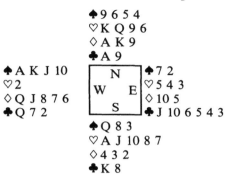

```
              ♠9 6 5 4
              ♡K Q 9 6
              ◇A K 9
              ♣A 9
♠A K J 10    ┌──────────┐   ♠7 2
♡2           │    N     │   ♡5 4 3
◇Q J 8 7 6   │ W     E  │   ◇10 5
♣Q 7 2       │    S     │   ♣J 10 6 5 4 3
             └──────────┘
              ♠Q 8 3
              ♡A J 10 8 7
              ◇4 3 2
              ♣K 8
```

East deals
None vulnerable

East	South	West	North
Pass	Pass	1 ◇	1 NT
Pass	3 ♡	Pass	4 ♡
All Pass			

Opening lead, Spade King

After West led the Spade King, dummy spread his cards. "If you like 9's," he smiled, "you're going to love this hand." It was an omen of things to come.

Declarer's survey showed four losers. His only chance seemed to be that his Spade Queen eventually would take a trick, so he silently prayed West would continue leading Spades and establish the concealed Queen.

On West's King, East signaled with the 7 and West did indeed continue the Ace. East's next card was the deuce. West shelled out the Spade Jack and East ruffed, dashing declarer's hope for a Spade trick.

The defenders now had their book. East returned the Diamond 10. Studying that spot and noting dummy's Diamond 9, declarer deduced East couldn't have a sequence, so he must have a doubleton Diamond or a singleton. Then the sun rose and illuminated the landscape.

West was busy in two suits! From the play it was obvious West held the Spade 10. He would have to keep holding it or dummy's Spade 9 would become a winner. From the bidding and from East's lead, West must also have long Diamonds, so dummy's Diamond 9 was threatening to become a winner. Both threat cards were in the same hand, but West was going to have to discard *before* dummy.

Thus it happened that an aura of confidence enveloped declarer. He won dummy's Diamond King, pulled trumps in two rounds, cashed out the two Club winners, and then started playing Hearts. With one more trump to go, this was the three-card position:

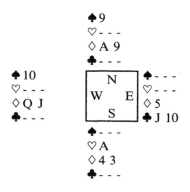

When the Heart Ace hit the table, it turned the screws on West. All West's cards were busy. He had to hold the Spade 10 because of dummy's 9, and he had to keep both Diamonds to stand over dummy's Diamond 9.

It didn't matter what West played. South had outgunned him with a squeeze maneuver, and South was winning the battle.

West suddenly developed a king-size headache which added to his plight. Finally he discarded a Diamond, so dummy let go of the Spade. Now the Diamond Ace smothered West's Queen and the Diamond 9 delivered the contract.

31. How to Succeed by Trying

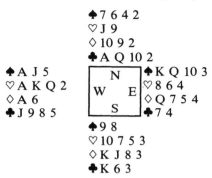

♠ 7 6 4 2
♡ J 9
◇ 10 9 2
♣ A Q 10 2

♠ A J 5
♡ A K Q 2
◇ A 6
♣ J 9 8 5

♠ K Q 10 3
♡ 8 6 4
◇ Q 7 5 4
♣ 7 4

♠ 9 8
♡ 10 7 5 3
◇ K J 8 3
♣ K 6 3

South deals
North-South vulnerable

South	West	North	East
Pass	1 Club	Pass	1 Spade
Pass	2 NT	Pass	3 NT
All Pass			

Opening lead, Club 2

When dummy appeared West counted his sure winners and found only eight, but he had several possibilities. One of his Clubs might win a trick, he might be able to sneak a trick with the Diamond Queen, or his long Heart might be established.

South won the opening lead with the Club King, returned a Club to North's 10, and North quickly snapped up the Ace-Queen. On the last Club South signaled with the Diamond 8, so North laid down the Diamond 10.

Declarer was in a quandary. The contract now appeared impossible unless the Heart deuce brought in a trick, a slim chance. The Odd-Even Rule said the six outstanding Hearts would probably split 4-2.

Refusing to capitulate, he planned his moves toward a squeeze. The opponents already had corrected the count for him, so he had the all-but-one situation. If South had the Diamond King and also had four Hearts, he could be subjected to a squeeze. The threat cards were dummy's Diamond Queen and his own Heart deuce.

Accordingly, declarer played a low Diamond from dummy, South echoed with the 3, and declarer won the Ace. Then West started running Spades. Here's the setup with one more Spade to go:

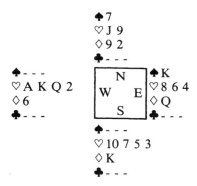

```
              ♠ 7
              ♡ J 9
              ◇ 9 2
              ♣ - - -
♠ - - -      ┌─────────┐    ♠ K
♡ A K Q 2    │    N    │    ♡ 8 6 4
◇ 6          │ W     E │    ◇ Q
♣ - - -      │    S    │    ♣ - - -
             └─────────┘
              ♠ - - -
              ♡ 10 7 5 3
              ◇ K
              ♣ - - -
```

The last Spade squeezed South. Protecting both red suits all by himself, he was in deep trouble. He was forced to discard a Heart.

Next declarer played a Heart and ran his Ace-King-Queen. All the defenders' Hearts fell and the lowly deuce was the game-going trick.

Note that Al Roth, with his fascinating foresight, would have beaten this contract, too. When he won the second Club trick, he would have led a Diamond. Now the count would not be rectified, so declarer would go down.

Perhaps someday Congress will pass a law to stop people like Roth from interfering — after we've learned to flimflam our enemy out of a winner in this simple fashion.

32. Betwixt and Between

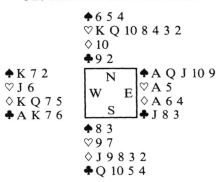

```
               ♠ 6 5 4
               ♡ K Q 10 8 4 3 2
               ◊ 10
               ♣ 9 2
  ♠ K 7 2           N        ♠ A Q J 10 9
  ♡ J 6        W        E    ♡ A 5
  ◊ K Q 7 5         S        ◊ A 6 4
  ♣ A K 7 6                  ♣ J 8 3
               ♠ 8 3
               ♡ 9 7
               ◊ J 9 8 3 2
               ♣ Q 10 5 4
```

West deals
East-West vulnerable

West	North	East	South
1 NT	3 ♡	3 ♠	Pass
4 ♠	Pass	4 NT	Pass
5 ◊	Pass	6 ♠	All Pass

Opening lead, Heart 9

Declarer found two losers in the master hand, a Club and a Heart. Looking for a place to deposit one of them, he realized it was possible to establish a long Diamond in dummy. Also there was a slim possibility the Club Queen was a doubleton, would fall on the Ace-King and establish the Jack. He decided to investigate both.

Winning the Heart Ace, he pulled trumps in three rounds, observing that North, who was obviously long in Hearts, was also long in Spades. This indicated South would probably have lots of Diamonds and Clubs and would be busy protecting both minors. Suddenly he became squeeze-minded.

Keenly aware he had two losers, he set out to correct the count. Right off he surrendered a Heart. North won and played another Heart. Declarer ruffed, South discarded a Diamond and dummy pitched a Club.

East cashed the Ace and King of Clubs, but the Queen did not appear. Then he played the King-Ace of Diamonds and North failed to follow. Yes, South was busy protecting Diamonds and Clubs and declarer had him in a vise. This was the situation:

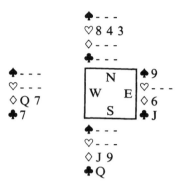

Declarer played the last trump. It was the squeeze card. South was in a jam. If he threw a Diamond, he set up dummy's long Diamond. If he threw the Club Queen, he was discarding a winner. Caught betwixt and between, he discarded the Club Queen.

Declarer cashed the ranking Jack of Clubs and then the Diamond Queen to bring in his ambitious slam.

IX. READING THE DUMMY

Just as a good detective has to think like a crook to ferret out clues, so a good defender has to think like a declarer to find his clues. The secrets of declarer's strategy are written in dummy and a defender can learn to read the messages.

When dummy comes down, while declarer is counting his tricks and looking for more, *make believe you're declarer and that's your dummy*. Start imagining how you'd use those 13 cards to the greatest advantage. Then, form a plan to foil declarer's use of dummy's strength. Your battle cry is: set this contract!

The dummy tells you whether you should wage:

- **An Active Defense:**
  Attacking dummy's entries, or
  Attacking dummy's trump holding, or
  Grabbing your winners quick.

- **A Passive Defense:**
  Letting declarer take the initiative, while you do nothing. Wait for tricks to come to you.

Keep in mind always how many tricks you need to put declarer down. Just knowing that number sharpens your wits and sparks your imagination. Count how many tricks you and partner have positively, and look around for other possibilities. Visualize what cards partner *might have* that would create extra winners.

Think positively! Believe that your side has the ammunition to win the battle.

There are three types of dummy, and each dictates a different defense: the dummy with a long, runnable side suit, the dummy with a short suit and ruffing power, and the dummy with neither a long suit nor ruffing power.

The Dummy with a Long Suit

When dummy has a long, easily established side suit, there's d-a-n-g-e-r ahead. Pursue an active defense. Strike out to kill dummy by knocking out its entries. If this appears impossible, grab your tricks quickly.

When the long suit is something like K-Q-J-x-x, Q-J-10-x-x, or A-J-10-x-x, try to kill dummy's entries, so that by the time that suit is established, declarer can't get over to use it.

However, when the long suit is A-K-Q-J-10, it's going to be almost impossible to kill dummy. It's obvious declarer is going to extract trumps, then run those winners and discard losers on them. This is an emergency! Rescue your tricks as quickly as you can before they burn up, and help partner get any he has, even if you have to lead from a dangerous holding like K-J-x-x or A-Q-x-x.

Here's an example where such a dummy set the sirens blaring:

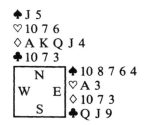

```
                   ♠ J 5
                   ♡ 10 7 6
                   ♦ A K Q J 4
                   ♣ 10 7 3
              ┌─────────────┐ ♠ 10 8 7 6 4
              │     N       │ ♡ A 3
              │  W     E    │ ♦ 10 7 3
              │     S       │ ♣ Q J 9
              └─────────────┘
```

South	West	North	East
1 ♡	Pass	2 ♦	Pass
2 ♡	Pass	4 ♡	All Pass

Opening lead, Club 5

West led the Club 5, dummy followed low, East played the Club 9 and South won the Ace. Then declarer brought out the Heart King. East took the Ace and cashed the Club Queen, partner following with the deuce.

Why don't you take over the East seat and manage the defense? Don your thinking cap! You have two tricks and you need two more. Dummy's advice is to take your winners quick. Are you going to try another Club or switch to a Spade?

The secret is knowing how many Clubs declarer has, and your partner just told you. When partner played the deuce on the second round he indicated he had five Clubs or two Clubs. If partner started with a doubleton, declarer started with five Clubs — and that doesn't make any sense on the auction. South would hardly rebid 2 Hearts with five Clubs in his hand.

It's obvious partner opened his fourth best Club and on the second round played the card under it. This means it's declarer who holds a doubleton. If you lead another Club, declarer will ruff, draw trumps, and run dummy's Diamonds.

Since you're wide-awake to analyses like these, you shift to a Spade to enable partner to collect any Spade tricks he might have. Take a look at what happens:

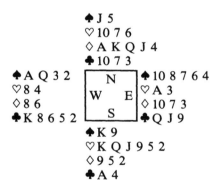

```
            ♠ J 5
            ♡ 10 7 6
            ◇ A K Q J 4
            ♣ 10 7 3
♠ A Q 3 2      N        ♠ 10 8 7 6 4
♡ 8 4       W     E     ♡ A 3
◇ 8 6          S        ◇ 10 7 3
♣ K 8 6 5 2            ♣ Q J 9
            ♠ K 9
            ♡ K Q J 9 5 2
            ◇ 9 5 2
            ♣ A 4
```

Your partner wins two Spades just in the nick of time and sets the contract. If declarer had the Spade Ace instead of the King, you wouldn't have gotten any more tricks, but it's more fun to die trying!

Sometimes the shift you need to make is dangerous, but bridge is not a game for the weak of heart. Maybe you'd like to test your courage on this one:

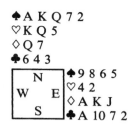

North	East	South	West
1 ♠	Pass	2 ♡	Pass
3 ♡	Pass	4 ♡	All Pass

Opening lead, Diamond 10

Sitting in the East chair, you win the first two Diamonds, and you see no more Diamond tricks are coming your way. You can't count on any Heart or Spade tricks, so your only hope for two more tricks lies in the Club suit. This is not difficult if your partner has the King.

However, you have 12 points in your own hand and the opponents have freely gone to game showing they have 26. So you sensibly conclude it's too much to expect that partner has the Club King. It is much more likely he has the Queen than the King. If partner has the Queen, there's hope of defeating the contract but not if you cash the Ace first!

This is where imagination comes in, and nerve, too. The play that gives you the best chance of stopping declarer is to lead the Club 2!

The whole hand was:

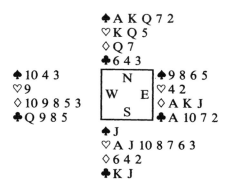

Since declarer has read you for the A-K-J of Diamonds, he's likely to place the Club Ace in your partner's hand and finesse the Jack. When partner wins the Queen, he returns a Club to your Ace and you earn a one-trick set.

If declarer had both the King and Queen of Clubs, you'd never get your Ace, and the opponents would score an extra 30 points. You ought to be willing to trade that overtrick for whatever small chance there might be of defeating the contract. An occasional set makes up for many lost Aces.

Why don't you move to the West seat now and try a little derring-do on this hand:

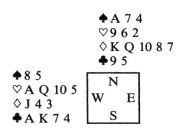

South	West	North	East
1 ♠	Double	3 ♠	Pass
4 ♠	All Pass		

Opening lead, Club King

You win the first trick with the Club King, East following with the 8. What's your plan?

Lots of players would take the Club Ace and the Heart Ace and throw in the sponge, but you're not a quitter.

You have three tricks in your hand and need one more. If you could get East on lead, he could send a Heart through declarer and sink this contract. Could East have the Diamond Ace? One thousand no's! Declarer has that card. The Diamond suit is coming in and declarer is going to pitch away his Heart losers.

Partner's Club 8 is a big card — the 3 and 2 are missing. Partner probably does not have a doubleton — that would leave declarer with five. The 8 looks like the beginning of a come-on signal. At the second trick suppose you lay down the Club 7. Look what happens:

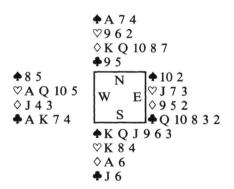

```
                    ♠ A 7 4
                    ♡ 9 6 2
                    ◇ K Q 10 8 7
                    ♣ 9 5
      ♠ 8 5          ┌─────────┐       ♠ 10 2
      ♡ A Q 10 5     │   N     │       ♡ J 7 3
      ◇ J 4 3        │ W     E │       ◇ 9 5 2
      ♣ A K 7 4      │   S     │       ♣ Q 10 8 3 2
                     └─────────┘
                    ♠ K Q J 9 6 3
                    ♡ K 8 4
                    ◇ A 6
                    ♣ J 6
```

East rises with the Club Queen and has no trouble finding the Heart switch. Declarer is in the glue before he even gets going.

Wait a minute! There's more to this story.

When this hand was actually played, the real East was a Thinker. He took his brain along when he went to the bridge table. He wondered to himself, "What if my partner needs me to force an honor out of declarer's hand?" *He shot back the Heart Jack!*

If declarer covered, he would lose three Heart tricks; if he didn't cover, East would hold the trick and thrust another Heart through. This imaginative play cost the poor declarer three Heart tricks for down two.

If East had played a low Heart, normally the correct card, declarer could have played low and West would win the 10, but West could rake in only one more Heart for down one.

Sometimes the defense has to abandon establishment of its own tricks in order to attack a vital entry in the dummy. Try the West seat again and read the road map in dummy showing the route declarer will take to make this contract:

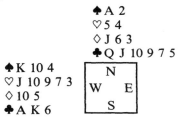

```
                    ♠ A 2
                    ♡ 5 4
                    ◇ J 6 3
                    ♣ Q J 10 9 7 5
    ♠ K 10 4        ┌─────────┐
    ♡ J 10 9 7 3    │    N    │
    ◇ 10 5          │  W   E  │
    ♣ A K 6         │    S    │
                    └─────────┘
```

South	West	North	East
1 NT	Pass	3 NT	All Pass

Opening lead, Heart Jack

After dummy comes down, there's a moment's pause. You are Detective West — what do you think South is planning to do?

Obviously declarer expects to win lots of tricks with dummy's Clubs. Even if you duck a round he can still get over with the Spade Ace. Then, whirling through your brain goes one command, "Kill that entry to dummy!" It doesn't take long to see you must sacrifice your Spade King to the glory of the cause.

South wins the first trick with the Heart King, but he's not fooling you. East is the person you trust and he played the Heart 2. East doesn't have the Heart Queen; declarer does. You can't set up your Hearts before declarer establishes his Clubs.

At trick two declarer plays a Club, just as you expected. You duck. After all, if declarer has three Clubs you'll have to concede one Club trick. Dummy's 9 wins. Declarer comes off dummy with a Diamond, winning the Queen.

Declarer plays another Club. You win the King and lay down the Spade King.* Now it's Katie Bar the Door! The whole hand:

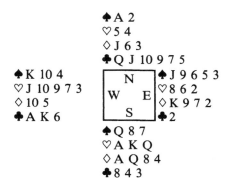

South has to win the Spade Ace. (If he ducked you'd just play another Spade.) Then, on the slim chance that the Diamond Jack will get him back to dummy, declarer next gives you the Club Ace.

You switch back to establishing Hearts. Declarer takes the Heart Ace and lays down the Diamond Ace, but the King won't fall. South has just run out of luck and dummy is as dead as a dodo bird. Eventually South limps in with two Spades, three Hearts, two Diamonds, and one Club, but he's one trick short of his contract because you took the time and trouble to read dummy.

---

* This play, the deliberate sacrifice of a high card with the object of knocking out a vital entry in an opponent's hand, is known as the Merrimac Coup. It is named after the *Merrimac,* an American ship sunk in 1898 in Santiago Harbor in an attempt to bottle up the Spanish fleet.

The Dummy with a Short Suit

When dummy has a short suit and it appears declarer will want to use dummy's trumps to ruff, pursue an active defense. It's urgent for the defenders to lead trumps at every opportunity to diminish dummy's ruffing power.

Some defenders don't like to lead trumps; they think that's doing declarer's work for him. Nevertheless, there are times when leading trumps is the killing defense. Look at this hand:

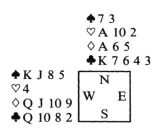

```
                    ♠ 7 3
                    ♡ A 10 2
                    ◇ A 6 5
                    ♣ K 7 6 4 3
        ♠ K J 8 5   ┌─────────┐
        ♡ 4         │ N       │
        ◇ Q J 10 9  │ W   E   │
        ♣ Q 10 8 2  │   S     │
                    └─────────┘
```

North	East	South	West
Pass	Pass	1 ♡	Pass
3 ♡	Pass	4 ♡	All Pass

Opening lead, Diamond Queen

Declarer wins the Diamond Ace and comes off dummy with a little Spade, East following with the 10 and the declarer the 2. As West, what are your thoughts?

You don't need a crystal ball to see that South wants to ruff a Spade in dummy. The time is ripe for the defenders to lead trumps. It's important for *you* to be the one to lead the suit because partner might have a trump honor and be embarrassed. (Besides, your partner might not be clever enough to conceive of that defense until you point it out.) So you hop up extravagantly with the Spade Jack, overtaking partner's 10, and bring forth a trump.

The whole shebang is:

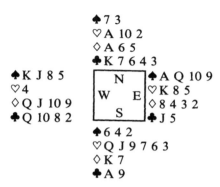

Declarer tries the trump finesse. East takes the King and — following the course you set — returns a Heart. Declarer wins and, making another valiant effort, plays another Spade. This time you play low, deliberately — you don't have a trump to lead, but partner probably does. Partner wins with the Spade 9 and snatches away dummy's last trump, torpedoing dummy's ruffing potential. Now declarer can never get a Spade ruff and has to settle for down one.

It was easy for you to diagnose that declarer couldn't set up dummy's long suit because you had Clubs bottled up. Your attack on trumps was bound to be the right defense. Your genius at reading dummy is bringing in dividends already!

Whenever dummy has a short suit, he often has a long suit, too, so the defenders have to consider what strategy to adopt — extract dummy's trumps, kill dummy's entries, or grab their own tricks.

Here's a famous hand from the 1932 Vanderbilt Team Championship. After three days of combat, the field narrowed to two teams for the finals. The score was so close the winner would be the side that earned a profit on this last hand. If the contract came in, North-South would win the title and the silver trophy; if East-West set the contract, they would get the laurels.

You take West's chair and see if you can snatch the title from your illustrious opponents — North, the wealthy Harold Vanderbilt, who created the game of contract from auction bridge, and South, his favorite partner, Waldemar Von Zedtwitz. In those bygone days bridge was a dressy affair and your fashionable opponents were attired in tails and white tie. The society editors hovered nearby.

On your toes! Your hand and dummy's were:

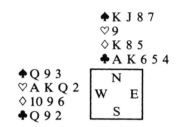

```
              ♠ K J 8 7
              ♡ 9
              ◇ K 8 5
              ♣ A K 6 5 4
  ♠ Q 9 3        ┌─────────┐
  ♡ A K Q 2      │    N    │
  ◇ 10 9 6       │ W     E │
  ♣ Q 9 2        │    S    │
                 └─────────┘
```

East	South	West	North
		1 ♡	Double
Pass	Pass		
2 ♡	3 ◇	Pass	4 ◇
Pass	5 ◇	All Pass	

Opening lead, Heart King

Your Heart King wins the first trick; you need two more. You ask yourself how, if you were Von Zedtwitz, would you use dummy?

If you think he wants to ruff Hearts, you lead trumps. If you think he can establish Clubs, you knock out dummy's Spade entry. If the case is hopeless, you grab your tricks quickly.

The 1932 West feared the Club suit was coming in, so he shifted to a Spade, trying to kill an entry. Von Zedtwitz put in the Jack and East won the Ace. The defenders now had their book.

Why don't you move over to the East chair and lead to trick three? Here's the whole hand, but don't let your eyes stray to the South cards:

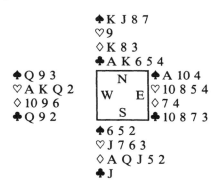

```
              ♠ K J 8 7
              ♡ 9
              ◇ K 8 3
              ♣ A K 6 5 4
♠ Q 9 3          N        ♠ A 10 4
♡ A K Q 2    W     E      ♡ 10 8 5 4
◇ 10 9 6                  ◇ 7 4
♣ Q 9 2          S        ♣ 10 8 7 3
              ♠ 6 5 2
              ♡ J 7 6 3
              ◇ A Q J 5 2
              ♣ J
```

East had two options. If he thinks the Clubs are coming in, he should follow partner's strategy and knock out dummy's Spade entry. The other choice is to use his final gasp by leading a trump to cut down Heart ruffs.

It was late at night and East was weary. He took the wrong route. He led a Heart, giving dummy a ruff! This shattered the defense.

Von Zedtwitz had been on tenterhooks, juggling imaginary places to ditch all those losers, but now he perked up. He ruffed the Heart in dummy, cashed the Club Ace, ruffed a second Club, ruffed a second Heart in dummy, and ruffed a third Club in his hand. The Queen toppled.

When Von Zedtwitz was deep in thought he invariably pulled his ear, a habit he eventually replaced, on medical advice, with twisting a lock of hair. At this moment he quit tugging his ear. He could see his contract coming in.

He extracted trumps with the Diamond A-Q-J and now had eight tricks. Since dummy still had the Spade King and the Club K-6 for winners, he claimed eleven tricks. Altogether he took five Diamonds in his hand, two ruffs in dummy, three Clubs and one Spade.

Both defenders had a chance to lower the boom. If West led a trump at trick two, Von Zedtwitz was doomed.

He couldn't manipulate all the things he had to do. He needed to get to his hand three different times, twice to play Hearts and once for the Spade finesse. It was more than he could manage.

At trick three East could have saved the day. If he shot back a Spade and knocked out the crucial dummy entry, Von Zedtwitz would have been down. No amount of ear-tugging would have helped.

Well, how did you do? Did you win the Vanderbilt? Sifting the evidence in dummy gives the clue.

The Balanced Dummy

When dummy has even distribution, no short suit for ruffing and no long suit to run, adopt a passive defense. Sit back and try to do nothing. Avoid initiating a new suit. Wait for the tricks to come to you.

If declarer can't ruff his losers in dummy and can't discard them on a long suit in dummy, some day he's going to have to play the suits in which he has losers. If you force declarer to break the suits, you'll catch bigger fish with your high cards.

There are certain ticklish card combinations* that cost the defenders a trick if they lead the suit first and cost declarer a trick if he leads it first. That's the reason behind the bridge bromide, "The side that breaks a suit averages a loss of half a trick in it."

---

* See Chapter VII, End Plays, under *Let the Opponents Help* for some of these combinations.

If you employ passive defense, you'll defeat this hand, but if you're aggressive, you won't:

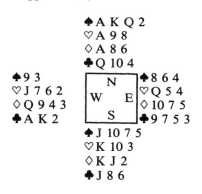

♠ A K Q 2
♡ A 9 8
◇ A 8 6
♣ Q 10 4

♠ 9 3
♡ J 7 6 2
◇ Q 9 4 3
♣ A K 2

♠ 8 6 4
♡ Q 5 4
◇ 10 7 5
♣ 9 7 5 3

♠ J 10 7 5
♡ K 10 3
◇ K J 2
♣ J 8 6

North	East	South	West
1 ◇	Pass	1 ♠	Pass
4 ♠	All Pass		

Opening lead, Club King

On West's Club King, East played the 3. Since West could see the 2 in his own hand he could interpret East's card as suggesting a switch. Luckily, West stopped to study dummy. With no long suits for discards and no short suits for ruffing, dummy dictated a passive defense. It appeared likely any shift would give declarer a trick he couldn't get on his own.

Accordingly, West continued the Ace of Clubs and then a third Club to dummy's Queen.

Declarer pulled trumps and tried the Diamond finesse, losing to West. Still not wishing to make any waves, West simply returned a Diamond. Declarer took two Diamonds and now had to break the Heart suit. He led the 10, West followed low, and so did dummy. East's Queen won. It was the setting trick.

Back up to trick two and let West shift to a new suit. If it's to a Diamond, declarer gets a free finesse and makes his game. If West shifts to a low Heart, declarer plays low from dummy, East has to rise with the Queen, and declarer takes the King. Now declarer can finesse West out of his Jack and never lose a Heart.

Take another look at the Heart suit and see why the defenders sometimes go into their shell and let the declarer break suits.

There is a way declarer can always make the hand if he forsees an endplay. Before reading on try to work it out.

First extract trumps. Now — since the Club suit has already been stripped from the North-South hands — strip the Diamonds. Cash the Ace-King and give up a Diamond. Refuse to finesse. Whoever wins has to concede a ruff-sluff or break the Heart suit. Either way South gets his game-going trick. There's more than one way to skin a cat!

Here's another endorsement for a passive defense:

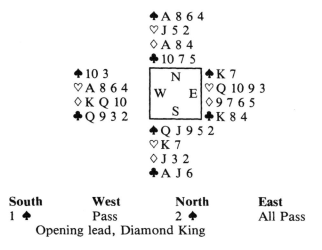

South	**West**	**North**	**East**
1 ♠	Pass	2 ♠	All Pass

Opening lead, Diamond King

When West led the Diamond King, dummy followed low, East played the 5, and declarer false-carded with the 3. West won the trick and had to make the next move.

West sensed the danger in continuing Diamonds; the declarer might be pulling the Bath Coup* on him. Since the set-up in dummy called for a passive defense, West didn't want to lead a Heart or a Club. He exited with a trump.

East won the King of Spades and played back a Diamond. Declarer followed low, so West's 10 forced the dummy's Ace. Declarer ran one more round of Spades to pull in the outstanding trumps.

Declarer didn't wish to initiate Clubs or Hearts either, so the struggle continued. He gave West his Diamond Queen, so now West was forced to break a new suit. He selected a low Club. East played the King and declarer won the Ace. Then South led back a low Club. West won the Queen and got out of the line of fire by returning a Club, declarer's Jack winning.

Now the burden of opening the Heart suit fell on declarer. He crossed to dummy with a trump and led a low Heart. East's 9 forced declarer's King and West took the Ace. Now West returned a Heart and East won the Queen. It was the sixth trick for the defenders so declarer was down one. He lost a Spade, two Hearts, two Diamonds, and a Club.

Try to familiarize yourself with these card combinations. Notice how unlucky it is to be the first to attack. If declarer had been the one to play the first Club and the defense was alert, South would have taken only one Club trick. He'd lead low from dummy and insert his Jack, losing to the Queen. Later when declarer has to lead the 10 from dummy, East covers with the King and forces South's Ace. Now West's 9 gets the third round. It was only because the defense had to break Clubs that declarer got two tricks.

Declarer had to break Hearts so he never got a Heart trick, but if either defender had led a Heart, declarer

---

* The Bath Coup is a hold-up of the Ace when the Jack is also held. If West continues the suit, declarer wins two tricks. If West leads the Queen, the Ace will take it and the Jack will be high. If West leads low, declarer will let it ride to the Jack. This card play dates back to the 1800's in the days of Whist and is believed named for the fashionable English watering place in Bath.

would always get a trick. If East leads a Heart, declarer plays low and West has to rise with the Ace to beat dummy's Jack. If West breaks Hearts, declarer easily makes the King.

Declarer Has a Hidden Suit

There is one type of hand where the proper defense is almost impossible to fathom — when declarer himself has a second suit but doesn't disclose it in the auction. The dummy might be calling for a passive game or a lead-trumps defense when the defenders really should be grabbing their tricks before they disappear on declarer's second suit.

That's why experienced declarers, receiving a raise in their first suit, conceal their second suit unless it's necessary to bid it to move toward a game or a slam.

Trump Promotion

Defenders can practice voodoo with their trumps when ruffing situations arise. The most obvious is the uppercut, a term borrowed from prizefighters. It's a ruff aimed at promoting a trump for partner. Here's how it works:

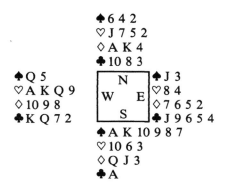

West	North	East	South
1 ♣	Pass	Pass	Double
Pass	1 ♡	Pass	2 ♠
Pass	3 ♠	Pass	4 ♠
All Pass			

Opening lead, Heart King

West wins the King-Queen-Ace of Hearts and is book-in. He continues another Heart. East strides into the center of the ring and uppercuts with the Spade Jack! This blow knocks the daylights out of South.

To keep from going down he has to overruff with the King, but when he does it promotes West's Queen into a winner. If East ruffs with a little card declarer has no problem; he overruffs with the Spade 7 and catches all the opposing trumps with the Ace-King.

A defender with a completely useless trump holding usually should ruff with his highest trump. Change West's Spades to the K-9-x or A-10-x. If East ruffs with the Jack, it builds up an extra trump trick for the defense. If West's holding is as sparse as the 10-x-x, the Jack ruff creates a winner.

It will help you anticipate uppercut opportunities if you lay out the above hand with a deck of cards and switch around these various trump holdings. You'll be fascinated watching the uppercut promote a card in partner's hand. You'll be even more fascinated someday watching it actually happen at the bridge table — with you delivering the blow.

More Trump Magic

Now let's stand behind the West chair and watch another stratagem promote a trump trick. This hand was dealt at a bridge party:

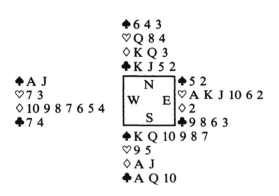

East	South	West	North
3 ♡	3 ♠	Pass	4 ♠
All Pass			

Opening lead, Heart 7

East won the opening Heart lead with the 10, cashed the King, and continued the Ace. Declarer was in a bind. If he ruffed low, West could overruff with the Jack, so declarer ruffed with the Queen. *West refused to overruff.* He discarded! This promoted a second trump trick for West. South's Queen won that trick, but later West's Ace-Jack trapped the King and West won both his honors, washing South's Spade game right down the drain.

Thus trump honors can increase in value when the holder plays *after* the declarer. Take this deal from a tournament:

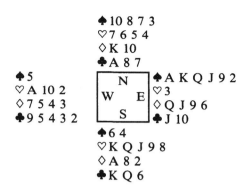

East	South	West	North
1 ♠	2 ♡	Pass	3 ♡
Pass	4 ♡	All Pass	

Opening lead, Spade 5

West led the Spade singleton, dummy followed low, and East won the 9. East returned the Spade Ace, again winning, and continued the Spade King. Now West had two trump tricks no matter what South did. If South ruffed with the Heart 8, West could overruff with the Heart 10 and, of course, he always would win the Ace.

However, South trumped with the King. West was tempted to capture the King with the Ace, but West was a cool cucumber. He reflected a moment and then threw away a Diamond. *By refusing to overruff* West later won two trump tricks. His Ace captured the Queen, the deuce went on the Jack, and the 10 became an assured winner.

When defending, watch for opportunities to promote your trumps and partner's. You'll find yourself playing against many unlucky declarers!

Reading the Dummy Drill

(1)

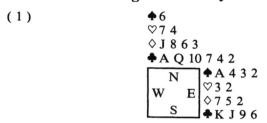

```
                    ♠ 6
                    ♡ 7 4
                    ◇ J 8 6 3
                    ♣ A Q 10 7 4 2
                ┌───────────┐    ♠ A 4 3 2
                │     N     │    ♡ 3 2
                │ W       E │    ◇ 7 5 2
                │     S     │    ♣ K J 9 6
                └───────────┘
```

South	West	North	East
1 ♡	1 ♠	Pass	2 ♠
3 ♡	Pass	4 ♡	All Pass

Opening lead, Spade King

Should East consider an active or passive defense? Why? What is his strategy?

(2)

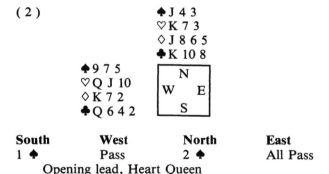

```
                    ♠ J 4 3
                    ♡ K 7 3
                    ◇ J 8 6 5
                    ♣ K 10 8
    ♠ 9 7 5    ┌───────────┐
    ♡ Q J 10   │     N     │
    ◇ K 7 2    │ W       E │
    ♣ Q 6 4 2  │     S     │
               └───────────┘
```

South	West	North	East
1 ♠	Pass	2 ♠	All Pass

Opening lead, Heart Queen

Dummy's King of Hearts covers the Queen, East wins the Ace and returns the suit. West takes the J-10. What should West lead at trick four? Why?

(3)

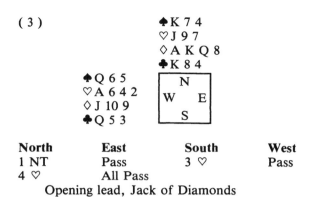

North	East	South	West
1 NT	Pass	3 ♡	Pass
4 ♡	All Pass		

Opening lead, Jack of Diamonds

Declarer wins the opening lead in dummy, East contributing the Diamond 2. Declarer leads a Heart to his King and West ducks. Next, a little Heart to dummy's Jack. Again West ducks, East discarding the Club deuce. On the third round of trumps West wins the Ace as East plays the Diamond 5.

What type of defense should West adopt? What should he play next?

(4)

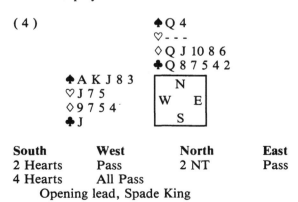

South	West	North	East
2 Hearts	Pass	2 NT	Pass
4 Hearts	All Pass		

Opening lead, Spade King

West wins the Spade King, Ace and Jack, partner and declarer following, so eleven Spades have been played. The defense needs one more trick. What's the best chance?

33. There Once Was a Dreamer

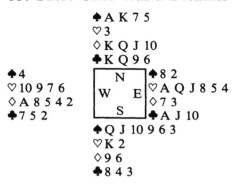

```
              ♠ A K 7 5
              ♡ 3
              ◇ K Q J 10
              ♣ K Q 9 6
♠ 4                         ♠ 8 2
♡ 10 9 7 6      N           ♡ A Q J 8 5 4
◇ A 8 5 4 2   W   E         ◇ 7 3
♣ 7 5 2         S           ♣ A J 10
              ♠ Q J 10 9 6 3
              ♡ K 2
              ◇ 9 6
              ♣ 8 4 3
```

North deals
None vulnerable

North	East	South	West
1 ◇	1 ♡	1 ♠	2 ♡
4 ♠	All Pass		

    Opening lead, Heart 10

In planning the defense, a defender is obliged to make optimistic assumptions. It can't possibly be right to give up — to assume the opponents' contract is impregnable. Many times it is because declarer simply has too much ammunition. Most of the time the battle is close and the outcome depends on how well each side handles its cards.

Consider this hand where East wins the Heart lead with his Ace. Declarer undoubtedly has the Heart King and a cursory glance at dummy shows there won't be any more Heart tricks for the defense.

East realizes partner has to have some values someplace for his raise, so East begins to consider where those values are. If West has a Spade honor, he'll never win a trick with it, so East dismisses that possibility.

The only Diamond honor missing from dummy's powerful suit is the Ace, so West must hold that card. That would give the defense a second trick and East's Club Ace is a third.

The defense needs one more trick to set the contract. The only place to find it is in Clubs. Then, East's imagination begins to click. He sees a way to set the contract — if partner has the Diamond Ace, and he just about has to.

That's how it happens that at trick two East leads the Club Jack! Declarer wins with dummy's Queen.

Declarer extracts trumps in two rounds and moves over to the Diamonds. After West takes the Ace, he leads the Club 7. East now holds the A-10 over dummy's K-9 and beats the hand a trick, a fine reward for a well-reasoned defense.

At trick two, if East plays any card other than the Club Jack, South easily glides in with his game.

Miraculously, everything worked out just as East planned. It just goes to show that some of your dreams will come true if you think hard and pray fervently.

34. The Pollyanna Play

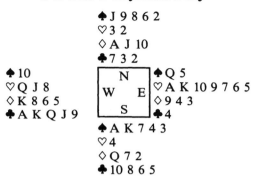

♠ J 9 8 6 2
♡ 3 2
◊ A J 10
♣ 7 3 2

♠ 10
♡ Q J 8
◊ K 8 6 5
♣ A K Q J 9

♠ Q 5
♡ A K 10 9 7 6 5
◊ 9 4 3
♣ 4

♠ A K 7 4 3
♡ 4
◊ Q 7 2
♣ 10 8 6 5

East deals
North-South vulnerable

East	South	West	North
3 ♡	Pass	4 ♡	All Pass

Opening lead, Spade King

After East preempted 3 Hearts, West carried on to
game. Looking admiringly at fine trump support and a
solid Club suit, he could envision a possible 12 tricks. Of
course he didn't consider a slam because of the shortage of
Aces.

South kicked off with the Spade King. Then dummy
hit the table, exposing to the world there'd be no more
Spade tricks for the defense and never, ever any Clubs.
Probably never any Hearts, either. The siren call was so
loud it almost pierced South's eardrums: "Grab your
Diamonds quick!"

South's Spade King captured the first trick, as North
signalled violently with the Spade Jack, a blatant suit-
preference signal for dummy's higher-ranking side suit, the
obvious Diamond shift. South stopped to scratch his head
and think.

The defense had one trick and the goal was to get
three more. How could Diamonds yield that many? Then

South made an unorthodox play. He put his finger on the Diamond Queen.

Quietly and on key, North began to hum the *Jubilate*. Declarer covered the Queen with the King (it didn't matter what he did). North won the Ace, cashed the Jack-10, and East was down one.

If South had led a low Diamond at trick two, the hand would have been made. Dummy could play low and North would win the 10. He could cash the Ace, but that would be the end of the road for the defense. Then East would be the one humming a happy tune.

It is almost always right to lead low from Q-7-2. All the experts do it; all the bridge authors preach it. Almost always, *but not always*. South could see he would never ever regain the lead. This was his final fling for the defense. If partner had the A-J-10, the Queen was the right card. If partner had only the A-J, the lead of the Queen wouldn't hurt anything.

The key to this defensive play, as well as to all defensive strategy, is the number of tricks needed, and the defenders needed three more. To believe partner had the A-J-10 was the Pollyanna approach, and that's the view the defenders have to take.

35. Just Sit in the Boat

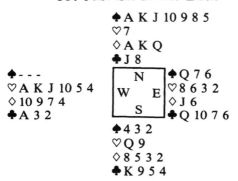

```
              ♠ A K J 10 9 8 5
              ♡ 7
              ◇ A K Q
              ♣ J 8
♠ - - -              ♠ Q 7 6
♡ A K J 10 5 4       ♡ 8 6 3 2
◇ 10 9 7 4           ◇ J 6
♣ A 3 2              ♣ Q 10 7 6
              ♠ 4 3 2
              ♡ Q 9
              ◇ 8 5 3 2
              ♣ K 9 5 4
```

South deals
East-West vulnerable

South	West	North	East
Pass	1 ♡	2 ♡	Pass
3 ♣	Pass	4 ♠	All Pass

Opening lead, Heart 2

North cue-bid the opponent's suit to show a strong hand, and after eliciting a Club response from partner, he leaped to a Spade game.

West won the opening Heart lead with the 10 and led the Heart King which declarer ruffed.

North laid down the Spade Ace and received a jolt when West was unable to follow. He cashed the Spade King and gave East his trump Queen.

The dummy told East what to play next and East heeded the advice. Since dummy was balanced, had no long suit, and offered no ruffing opportunities, he played passively. East returned a Heart and let declarer ruff again. Declarer led a couple of rounds of trumps, but this caused no problems for the defenders. West had plenty of Hearts to throw and East shed a Heart and a Club.

Finally declarer had to broach the Club suit himself. He led the 8, East covered with the 10, forcing dummy's King, and West won the Ace. Then West returned a Heart and declarer trumped with his last trump. He took his three Diamonds but on the last trick had to concede a Club to East's Queen. That was the setting trick.

Many Easts, after winning the trump Queen, would get apprehensive about their tricks, and would break Clubs. This would gum up the defense. Declarer would play low from dummy and West would either have to go up with his Ace, establishing dummy's King for the game-going trick, or permit declarer's Jack to win. As long as the defenders refused to break the Club suit, North was sure to go down.

Most of us, accustomed to blasting into the wild blue yonder looking for tricks, can hardly bear to sit back and wait for them to come to us. It's tough to twiddle your thumbs.

Like the gardener who over-fertilizes the plants he cherishes, we often overdo in bridge, losing a trick that is our rightful heritage. There are times when it's best to be aggressive and there are times when it's best to be passive. The wisdom of which to be when is written in dummy.

36. The Power of Positive Thinking

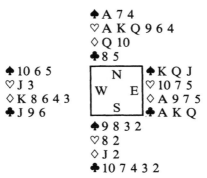

```
                    ♠ A 7 4
                    ♡ A K Q 9 6 4
                    ♢ Q 10
                    ♣ 8 5
      ♠ 10 6 5          ┌─────────┐         ♠ K Q J
      ♡ J 3             │    N    │         ♡ 10 7 5
      ♢ K 8 6 4 3       │  W   E  │         ♢ A 9 7 5
      ♣ J 9 6           │    S    │         ♣ A K Q
                        └─────────┘
                    ♠ 9 8 3 2
                    ♡ 8 2
                    ♢ J 2
                    ♣ 10 7 4 3 2
```

West deals
All vulnerable

West	North	East	South
Pass	1 ♡	Double	Pass
2 ♢	2 ♡	4 ♢	All Pass

Opening lead, Heart King

North cashed the King of Hearts and continued the Queen, everyone following suit. North noted South played the 8, then the 2 to signal a doubleton. Then North collected the Spade Ace and the defenders were book-in.

Looking at dummy's impressive Spades and Clubs, North realized the contract could not be defeated unless the defenders scored a trump trick. Accordingly, at trick four, North led the Heart 4, in effect asking South to uppercut the trick with his highest trump. This was very productive. South duly obliged by ruffing with the Jack.

This pulled the rug out from under the declarer. West now had to lose a trump trick and go down one, rewarding North-South for their first-class defense.

If South had ruffed with the deuce, declarer would have had no trouble. He'd simply overruff with the 3, and then the A-K would bring in the adverse trumps. South's Jack was useless anyway, so he spent it to force an honor from declarer, hoping to establish some card for his partner.

A defender sees only his own hand and dummy, but he should constantly consider and reconsider what cards partner could have to defeat the contract. It should be an automatic reflex to credit partner with a crucial card. The old tune carries a message for defenders, "Accentuate the positive; eliminate the negative."

X. THE NEGATIVE DOUBLE

There once was a day when there was only one kind of double; when a player said "double" he meant he could set the opponents. It was always a penalty double. In 1913, a bridge genius came along and created the "take-out" double, adding an exciting new dimension to bidding and a great zest to the game. It is probably the most strategically valuable call in bridge.

After that the double of a low-level bid asked partner to name his best suit, any one of the unbid suits, with one exception: if your partner had already made a bid, the double was for penalties.

South	West	North	East
(1) 1 ♣	Double		
(2) 1 ♣	Pass	1 ♠	Double
(3) 1 ♣	Pass	Pass	1 ♡
Double			

In (1) West made a take-out double asking East to bid a Spade or a Heart or a Diamond, whichever was his best suit. In effect, West made an overcall in three suits with one bid. In (2) East made a take-out double asking West to bid Hearts or Diamonds. In (3) South reopened the bidding with a take-out double, asking North to name his best suit — Spades, Clubs, or Diamonds. As you see, this valuable take-out double is available to everyone at the table *except poor North, the partner of the opener*.

In 1957, another bridge genius came along, Alvin Roth, and rescued North. He designed a third use for the double. He called his bid "the negative double". The object was to add a take-out double to the repertoire of the *responder*. This negative double is available to only one person at the table — the partner of the opening bidder.

After an opening bid, if an opponent intervenes with a low-level overcall, a double by responder is "negative". It means just what the name implies. The bid says, "This is a 'negative' double. I don't mean it as a penalty double. I want you to take me out of it by bidding a new suit. I have some values but I don't wish to play in the suit you opened."

Thus the partner of the opening bidder is given a take-out double — a way that he, too, can ask his partner to bid some other suit.

Everyone using ordinary take-out doubles is familiar with the importance of support for unbid major suits. The same principle applies to the negative double. If there is one unbid major, the negative double guarantees four cards in that major, and if there are two unbid majors, the negative double guarantees four cards in both majors.

Rescuing the Heart Suit

The most common sequence is the one that rescues the Heart suit:

South	West	North	East
1 ♣	1 ♠	Double	

North's hand might be:

(A)	♠ x x	(B)	♠ x x	(C)	♠ x x
	♡ K J x x		♡ A K J x		♡ K Q x x
	◊ A x x x		◊ A Q x x x		◊ A Q 10 x
	♣ x x x		♣ x x		♣ x x x

North in effect has said, "I bid 1 Heart," and South rebids accordingly just as though West had not overcalled and North had been able to bid 1 Heart:

With 13-15 and four cards in Hearts, "2 Hearts".
With 16-18 and four cards in Hearts, "3 Hearts".
With 19-21 and four cards in Hearts, "4 Hearts".

Why didn't North just come out and bid 2 Hearts? Because bidding Hearts at the 2-level promises five cards in the suit and at least 10 points. Lacking either condition, the responder may utilize the negative double.

In (A) North used the negative double with a minimum responding hand. If South rebids 2 Hearts, North passes. However, if South's rebid is a jump to 3 Hearts, North — with a hand valued at 9 points — accepts the invitation and bids game.

With (B) the negative double is used with a full opening bid. If partner rebids 2 Hearts, North jumps to game.

With (C) North is in-between. If partner rebids 2 Hearts, North invites game with 3 Hearts.

The negative double also brings relief in another awkward situation.

South	West	North	East
1 ♣	1 ♠	Double	Pass
2 ♣	Pass	2 ♡	

North's negative double promised four Hearts, and South's rebid of 2 Clubs denied four Hearts. When North then bid Hearts on his own, he showed a strong five-card suit or a six-card suit. Obviously he had the length to come in originally but not the strength. This shows a weak hand and is not forcing. The hand might be:

(D) ♠ x x
    ♡ A Q x x x x
    ◇ x x x
    ♣ x x

(E) ♠ x x
    ♡ A Q J x x
    ◇ x x x
    ♣ x x x

Describing Your Spades

The negative double is also valuable in helping the Spade suit surface as trumps. Here are some possibilities:

South	West	North	East
(1) 1 ♣	1 ♡	Double	

The negative double shows four Spades. Example: ♠ KJxx ♡ xx ◇ KJxx ♣ xxx. If North comes in freely with 1 Spade he has a five-card suit. Thus the negative double enables the partnership to distinguish between a four-card

and a five-card Spade suit after a 1 Heart overcall.
This auction might continue:

South	West	North	East
1 ♣	1 ♡	Double	Pass
1 ♠	Pass	2 ♠	Pass

South's rebid shows four Spades and a minimum opener of 13-15, and North's single raise shows four Spades and a minimum responding hand of 6-9. Here North could afford to confirm the trump fit because the auction had only reached the 1-level. The 2 Spade bid also has preemptive value, making it harder for the opponents to enter the auction.

South	West	North	East
(2)1 ♣	1 ♢	Double	

The negative double shows four cards in both majors. North's hand might be: ♠ QJxx ♡ AJxx ♢ xx ♣ Jxx.

Coming in with one major does not deny four cards in the other major. Holding ♠ QJxx ♡ AJxxx ♢ xx ♣ Jx, bid 1 Heart to show five cards. This gives partner an option of raising Hearts with three-card support or bidding Spades.

Suppose you had only *one* of the majors. There is disagreement among the experts, but you and your partner can have an understanding about what you want to do. One way is to bid your major at the 1-level but let partner beware that you might have only four cards in the suit. Example: ♠ KJxx ♡ xxx ♢ KJxx ♣ xx.

South	West	North	East
(3) 1 ♡	2 ♣	Double	

The negative double shows North has Spades and Diamonds and wants South to choose between the unbid suits. His hand might be:

(F)	♠ K Q x x	(G)	♠ K x x x x
	♡ x x		♡ x x
	◇ A Q x x x		◇ A J x x
	♣ x x		♣ x x

With (F) the Spade suit isn't long enough to come into the bidding; with (G) the Spade suit is long enough but the hand isn't strong enough to name a new suit at the 2-level. The negative double solves both dilemmas.

How About the Minors?

When both major suits have been bid, the negative double asks partner to choose a minor:

South	West	North	East
1 ♠	2 ♡	Double	

North's negative double shows support in both minors and asks South to choose one of them. His hand might be ♠ xx ♡ xx ◇ QJxxx ♣ AKxx. North doesn't have a Spade raise. Naturally, anyone would rather play Spades than Diamonds or Clubs.

North isn't strong enough to bid one minor now and the other on the next round. The negative double enables him to show both suits with one bid.

How Many Points?

How good a hand do you need to make a negative double? When South, your partner, opens the bidding and West overcalls, the auction has been kept alive for South. If South has a rock-crusher he's going to get another chance to bid. Therefore, as North, you needn't strain to bid with a bad hand, a mere 5 points or a bad 6.

Using the negative double implies a minimum responding hand of 6-9 points. If you have more, you bid again.

There is no upper limit because the object of the negative double is to probe for the best trump suit.

The important question is, "How high are you pushing the auction?" If your partner can rebid at the 1-level (Example: South — 1 ◇, West — 1 ♡, You — Double), or at the 2-level (Example: South — 1 ◇, West — 1 ♠, You — Double), all you need is 6 points. When you're pushing the auction to the 3-level (Example: South — 1 ◇, West — 2 ♠, You — Double), you need 10.

How High?

How high can the overcall be and the negative double still apply? You and your partner can limit the negative double to any level you like. You might wish to start using negative doubles only after a 1 Spade overcall to show four cards in the Heart suit. Later, after you've tested the waters and are more comfortable with the bid, move forward and include 2-level overcalls. Most experts play the negative double through 3 Spade overcalls.

The Penalty Double

Suppose you want to make a penalty double but you are playing the negative double, what can you do? Let's say your partner opens a Diamond, the next player jumps to 2 Spades, and you want to crack it with a penalty double because you hold ♠ AJ9xx ♡ Kxx ◇ x ♣ Qxxx.

You have a perfect penalty double, but don't double! Be patient. Pass.

To cover the possibility that you were prevented from making a penalty double because you are playing negative doubles, the opener must make every effort to reopen the bidding with a double. The shorter the opener's Spades, the more chance there is partner is just waiting for a reopening double so he can pass and convert it to a penalty double. This is a vital part of the negative double.

In this way you have the best of both worlds — the immediate negative double for take-out and the reopening double that can be converted into an old-fashioned penalty double.

If the auction goes:

South	West	North	East
1 ◇	2 ♣	Pass	Pass
?			

and South holds ♠Axx ♡KJxx ◇KQxxx ♣x, South should reopen with a double because it is likely the responder is long in Clubs and wanted to make a penalty double. However, with Clubs and Spades reversed, it is less likely North has Clubs and more likely he passed because he was weak, so there is less obligation to reopen with a double.

When a responder makes a negative double, the opener also has an option to pass for penalties. Suppose the auction goes:

South	West	North	East
1 ♠	2 ♡	Double	Pass
?			

and the opener holds ♠KQ10xx ♡KQ10x ◇Ax ♣xx. North is obviously asking South to bid Diamonds or Clubs but the opener may choose to pass for penalties. Thus users of the negative double can inflict a penalty double from either side.

It's an Alert

When a player makes a negative double, his partner says, "Alert!" before the next player has a chance to bid. That is a way to say, "My partner has just made an unusual bid which is a convention."

South, "1 Club"
West, "1 Spade"
North, "Double"
South, "Alert"

East is entitled to ask the meaning of the bid if he so desires, and if he does ask, South briefly describes the bid, explaining the double is not for penalties but is for take-out.

The negative double is the most popular and the most startling performer of all new conventions. After Blackwood and Stayman, it is the most important bidding convention in bridge. It has been adopted by 90% of the duplicate world.

When Roth first designed the negative double, pioneers trying it fondly called it Sputnik. The Russians had just launched their Sputnik into outer space, and this bidding convention helped a player get his suit into orbit in competitive auctions.

You and your favorite partner may want to begin using the negative double only over 1 Spade to show four cards in the Heart suit. However, on these lesson hands, practice using the negative double through the level of 3 Spades.

Negative Double Drill

(1) As North, what would you call with each hand?

South	West	North	East
1 ◇	1 ♠	?	

(a)	(b)	(c)	(d)
♠ xx	♠ Kx	♠ xx	♠ xx
♡ KJxx	♡ KQJx	♡ Kxxx	♡ AQxxxx
◇ Axxx	◇ Axxxx	◇ Jxx	◇ xxx
♣ xxx	♣ xx	♣ Jxxx	♣ xx

(2) As North, what would you bid with these?

South	West	North	East
1 ♣	1 ♡	?	

(a)	(b)	(c)	(d)
♠ K10xx	♠ KQ10x	♠ xx	♠ KJxxx
♡ xxx	♡ x	♡ AQ10xxx	♡ x
◇ KJxx	◇ xxx	◇ KQJx	◇ xxx
♣ Qx	♣ AQ10xx	♣ x	♣ AQxx

(3) As North, what would you say with these?

South	West	North	East
1 ♣	1 ◇	?	

(a)	(b)
♠ Q10xx	♠ KJxxx
♡ A10xx	♡ KJxx
◇ xx	◇ xx
♣ Jxx	♣ xx

(4) As South, what's your rebid?

South	West	North	East
1 ♣	1 ♠	Double	Pass
?			

(a)	(b)	(c)	(d)
♠ xx	♠ Ax	♠ AJ10x	♠ xx
♡ KJxx	♡ KJxx	♡ xx	♡ Axxx
◇ Axx	◇ xx	◇ Kxx	◇ Kxx
♣ KQxx	♣ AKQxx	♣ AQxx	♣ AKQx

37. Rescuing the Heart Suit

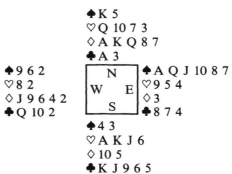

```
              ♠ K 5
              ♡ Q 10 7 3
              ◇ A K Q 8 7
              ♣ A 3
♠ 9 6 2                          ♠ A Q J 10 8 7
♡ 8 2          N                 ♡ 9 5 4
◇ J 9 6 4 2  W   E               ◇ 3
♣ Q 10 2       S                 ♣ 8 7 4
              ♠ 4 3
              ♡ A K J 6
              ◇ 10 5
              ♣ K J 9 6 5
```

North deals
North-South vulnerable

North	East	South	West
1 ◇	2 ♠	Double*	Pass
4 ♡	Pass	5 ♡	Pass
6 ♡	All Pass		

*Negative Double

Opening lead, Spade Ace

After the dealer opened a Diamond, East made a weak jump overcall of 2 Spades. This could have thrown a monkey wrench into the North-South bidding machinery, making it almost impossible to find the Heart fit, but North and South knew a convention that protected them against such Machiavellian preempts.

South said, "Double". It was the modern and effective negative double. (North echoed, "Alert!") South's double was, in effect, a take-out double asking North to bid again.

Since South's negative double guaranteed four cards in the unbid major, Hearts, North knew just what to do for he also held four Hearts. A trump suit had been discovered! With a maximum opener, North leaped forthwith to 4 Hearts.

Then South, deciding his hand was worth one more move, called, "5 Hearts," suggesting a slam if North had first or second round control of Spades. North accepted with alacrity.

On lead with no attractive choice, East kicked off with the Spade Ace, winning trick one, as West contributed the 2. East played another Spade to declarer's King.

Declarer extracted trumps in three rounds. To his surprise he found East, who was obviously long in Spades, also held three Hearts.

Moving right along declarer, with two long suits, had to establish one. Beginning with the stronger, he cashed the Diamond Ace, then the King. On the second round East couldn't follow. Alas, the Diamond suit wouldn't bring in the slam.

There was nothing to do but try Clubs. Stopping to reflect, North pondered on the distribution of that suit. He held seven Clubs, the opponents six. How were those six divided?

Since he knew more about East's hand, he began to count East's distribution. The bidding and the play suggested six Spades, three Hearts and one Diamond. That left three cards in the Club suit. The outstanding Clubs were split 3-3! He didn't need to risk the finesse because he could ruff out the Queen. Counting had cleared away the clouds.

He laid down the Club Ace, crossed to dummy's King, and led a third round. The Queen appeared and North ruffed as the suit came romping in. Declarer cashed the Diamond Queen, trumped a Diamond in dummy, and brought out dummy's Club Jack for his slam-going trick. He won five trump tricks, three Diamonds, three Clubs, and a Spade.

Actually, the hero was the negative double, which helped North-South find their 4-4 fit in Hearts. Without that helpful convention they were heading for *The Wreck of the Hesperus*. North can't make 5 Diamonds, South can't make 5 Clubs, and who wants to languish in 3 No Trump when he can score 6 Hearts!

38. Why Fish in Dangerous Waters?

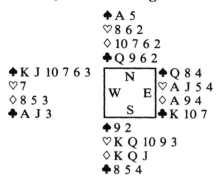

♠ A 5
♡ 8 6 2
♢ 10 7 6 2
♣ Q 9 6 2

♠ K J 10 7 6 3
♡ 7
♢ 8 5 3
♣ A J 3

♠ Q 8 4
♡ A J 5 4
♢ A 9 4
♣ K 10 7

♠ 9 2
♡ K Q 10 9 3
♢ K Q J
♣ 8 5 4

East deals
East-West vulnerable

East	South	West	North
1 ♢	1 ♡	1 ♠	2 ♡
2 ♠	Pass	4 ♠	All Pass

Opening lead, Heart 8

Since East and West were employing the negative double, West's free bid of a Spade guaranteed five cards in the suit. With only four he would use the negative double. Consequently, East had no problem surfacing with a Spade raise despite holding only three cards in the suit.

After the raise West re-evaluated his hand, adding a point for his fifth trump and two for his sixth. This shot his values up to 14, so he contracted for the Spade game.

When dummy came down declarer stopped to take inventory and found four losers in the master hand — a trump, two Diamonds, and a Club. The only one he could do anything about was the Club. He absolutely had to locate the Club Queen.

Winning the opening lead with dummy's Heart Ace, declarer began to set up an endplay to force an opponent to lead Clubs for him. He came off dummy with a Heart, ruffing in his hand.

Then he brought out the Spade King. North took the Ace and switched to a Diamond. Declarer won dummy's Ace and led a third round of Hearts, ruffing with the Spade 10.

Next, West played a Spade to dummy's Queen and the outstanding trumps tumbled in. He led dummy's last Heart, again ruffing. This wiped out dummy's Hearts. He led a low Diamond and South, perforce, won the King and took the Queen.

South was in the spotlight and the drama of the next card was about to unfold. Reduced to four cards, a Heart and three Clubs, he had to concede declarer a ruff-sluff or open up Clubs. He chose a Club. Declarer ducked, North rose with the Queen, and dummy's King won. All the rest belonged to declarer. He took five Spades, one Heart, one Diamond, and three Clubs.

East's refusal to go fishing for the Club Queen was an expert play. Why should he plunge headlong into those perilous waters when, with a little skill, he could force an opponent to hook the Queen for him!

39. All Aboard the Twentieth Century!

By Becky Levering

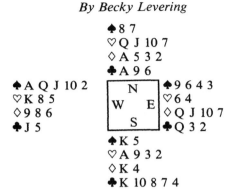

```
              ♠ 8 7
              ♡ Q J 10 7
              ◇ A 5 3 2
              ♣ A 9 6
♠ A Q J 10 2      N         ♠ 9 6 4 3
♡ K 8 5      W       E      ♡ 6 4
◇ 9 8 6          S          ◇ Q J 10 7
♣ J 5                       ♣ Q 3 2
              ♠ K 5
              ♡ A 9 3 2
              ◇ K 4
              ♣ K 10 8 7 4
```

South deals
All vulnerable

South	West	North	East
1 ♣	1 ♠	Double*	2 ♠
3 ♡	Pass	4 ♡	All Pass

*Negative Double

Opening lead, Diamond 9

Every now and then in the history of bridge someone comes along with a new bid that solves problem hands and brings in bushels of points. Such is the modern negative double. It is especially valuable to people playing five-card majors because it helps locate the valuable 4-4 trump fit.

When West overcalled a Spade he could have put North in an awkward situation. With 11 high-card points he certainly wanted to enter the auction, but how could he? If he bids Hearts at the 2-level he would promise five cards. Luckily, he could use the negative double to show his four Hearts and to elicit another bid from partner.

South was on target. He rebid 3 Hearts, revealing he, too, held four cards in that major and describing a minimum opener.

Now North went to 4 Hearts. West opened a Diamond.

Declarer counted four losers in the master hand — two Spades, a Heart, and at least one Club. He quickly noted he had a dangerous opponent. East was the villain. If East ever won the lead, he'd shoot a Spade through South's K-5 and the game would go down the chute. Right off he planned his maneuvers to keep East on the sidelines.

Winning the opening Diamond in dummy, declarer led the Heart Queen and finessed. West won the King and returned another Diamond. Declarer's King won. He pulled trumps with the Jack and the 10.

Now South set out to develop his Club suit, leading dummy's Club 9. When East followed low, so did declarer, and West won the Jack. It was the second trick for the defense.

West played another Diamond and declarer ruffed with his very last trump, the Ace. South led a Club to the Ace and, when everyone followed, the contract was assured. A Club to the King cleared the suit and South cashed two Club winners, throwing away dummy's two Spades.

He led a Spade and trumped with dummy's last Heart, which gave him his tenth trick. Dummy still had a Diamond left so East finally won a trick but it was too late to thrust through a Spade.

Suppose for a moment declarer had carelessly cashed the Ace-King of Clubs, planning to concede the third round to anybody who happened to hold the Queen. East would win and shoot a Spade through, and West would take two Spades to set the contract.

Nevertheless, the hand was easier to play than to bid, unless you happen to have the valuable negative double up your sleeve. Then it's just a game of pat-a-cake.

If you and your bridge club aren't playing the negative double, it's time to hop aboard the bandwagon with today's scientific bidders. When you run into a snag, don't be discouraged. You can't start out being perfect. Discuss your mix-ups; re-read the explanations. There's better bidding in your future!

40. You Can Have Your Cake!

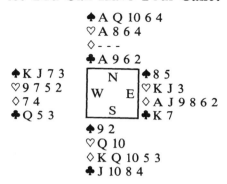

♠ A Q 10 6 4
♡ A 8 6 4
◇ - - -
♣ A 9 6 2

♠ K J 7 3
♡ 9 7 5 2
◇ 7 4
♣ Q 5 3

♠ 8 5
♡ K J 3
◇ A J 9 8 6 2
♣ K 7

♠ 9 2
♡ Q 10
◇ K Q 10 5 3
♣ J 10 8 4

West deals
None vulnerable

West	North	East	South
Pass	1 ♠	2 ◇	Pass
Pass	Double	Pass	Pass
All Pass			

Opening lead, Spade 9

Using the negative double you can have your cake and eat it too. You can still make penalty doubles of low-level contracts providing you and your partner understand the ground rules. This hand illustrates the technique.

After North opened a Spade, East overcalled 2 Diamonds. Now South longed to lower the ax and make a penalty double, but he couldn't. He and his partner were using the negative double bidding convention and a double here would be for take-out, asking North to bid a new suit — Hearts or Clubs. That was not what South wanted, so he had to be disciplined and say, "Pass".

When the auction circled back to North, there was a call he was duty-bound to make. He had to re-open the bidding with a double in case partner had wished to make a penalty double. After North said, "Double," East passed, South passed with pleasure, and West passed.

South kicked off with the Spade 9, dummy's Jack covered, and North won the Queen, cashed the Ace and continued a third round. On this declarer discarded a Heart and South trumped.

South brought forth the Club Jack, North signaled with the 6, and declarer won the King. Then East laid down the trump Ace and, to his horror, saw North unable to follow. From then on the hand was a blur, but East did the best he could. Abandoning trumps, he led a Club and put up dummy's Queen, losing to North's Ace.

North pulled out another Club, which declarer ruffed to win. Declarer now held ♡K-J ◇J-9-8-6. Not caring to lead a Heart from that holding, he played another Diamond. South won the 10, cashed the King and Queen, and exited with his last Club. Declarer ruffed with his last trump and — to add to his woes — finally had to break Hearts. He laid down the Jack; South won the Queen and then gave North the Heart Ace.

The defenders took two Spade tricks, four Diamonds, two Hearts and one Club. That spelled down four and North-South amassed 700 points.

Looking back, there wasn't anything wrong with East's overcall. He was just unlucky to find South with the trumps bunched over him. However, give North-South credit. They made the most of East's bad draw. Notice how careful the defenders were not to lead Hearts, because if they had declarer could turn one more trick.

After North reopened the bidding with a double, what would South have done if he hadn't held such a fistful of Diamonds? He'd have to bid, so he'd probably call 2 Spades.

ANSWERS FOR DRILLS

John Bennett's Errors

In keeping with the principle of preserving entries to the hand with the long suit, (1) Bennett first should have cashed the Spade King in his own hand. (2) Finesse West, who doubled, for the trump Queen. (3) Pull all trumps. Take the Club Ace and run Clubs until East rises with the Queen, then ruff. (4) Now's the time to ruff a Diamond and reach dummy to play the established Clubs. This way Bennett winds up with six trumps tricks and four Clubs to make the game and save his life. It Pays to Plan the Play!

I. Planning

(1) (a) Probably fourth best. The Diamond honors are divided.

(b) Four Spades, four Hearts, one Diamond, two Clubs, and two or three Diamond ruffs — 13 or 14 winners.

(c) Six losers — three Aces and three small Diamonds.

(d) Counting losers was faster and also gave a more realistic view of the hand.

(e) Throw Diamond losers on dummy's long Spades.

(f) The problem in this hand is to avoid losing a Diamond trick. Do not try to ruff out the Diamonds! When an opponent wins one of the black Aces he might play the Heart Ace and lead another Heart and dummy will be too short of trumps to take care of the Diamonds. First, *set up the Spade suit while you have trumps in dummy to stand guard over Diamond returns*. Then pull trumps and run your Spades.

(2) (a) Top of sequence in honors.

(b) Four, one Diamond and three Clubs.

(c) Win the Club Ace, play the King of Spades and then the Ace-Queen, discarding one of dummy's Clubs. Give up a Club. If the opponent returns a trump (best), win it in your hand and lead a Club. Ruff with an honor so no one can overruff. Cash dummy's trump. Give up a Diamond. When you regain the lead, pull trumps. This gives you 6 Heart tricks, 3 Spades, and 1 Club = 10.

(3)   (a) Probably long suit. Probably doesn't have the Queen.

        (b) Four Spades, two Hearts, two Diamonds, one Club = 9.

        (c) There is a problem reaching the South hand to collect the Queen-Jack of Spades.

        (d) The best place to find more tricks is to establish the long Diamonds. You have eight; the opponents have five. If they split 3-2 you get three more Diamond tricks. *This gives you the contract if you can reach South's Spade tricks*. Spurn the Heart finesse at trick one; this preserves the Heart King as an entry to the Spade Queen-Jack.

        (e) The play goes: win the Heart Ace, unblock Spades by playing the Ace and King, then lead a low Diamond and duck. Win any return. If East should win the Diamond and play back a Heart, refuse the finesse; it's too dangerous. Run up with the King, cash your Spade honors, then go over to dummy's Diamonds. You get four Spades, two Hearts, five Diamonds, one Club = 12.

II. Trump Management

(1)   (a) Win Heart Ace and go after trumps. Keep leading trumps until you have taken all the opponents', then run your Diamond suit. You expect 11 tricks — five Diamonds, four Clubs, and two Aces. The danger is someone might ruff a Diamond.

        (b) Win the Spade Ace and pull two rounds of trumps with the Queen and the Ace. Now set up the Club suit, retaining the trump King as the entry to reach dummy's Clubs, in the event the opponent with the Club Ace holds up. You risk a Club ruff with that outstanding trump, but it's your only hope.

(2) It's a crossruff. Win the Spade 7, cash the Club Ace, then the Heart Ace and crossruff the hand, trumping Diamonds in dummy and Hearts in the closed hand. You'll garner 10 tricks, eight trumps and two Aces.

(3) Win the Heart Ace and immediately play the A-K-Q of Diamonds to discard one Heart loser; then go after trumps. The opponents have to get their two Aces and you can't afford to lose two Hearts also.

(4) Pave the way for a ruffing trick by discarding in dummy. Win the Heart in your hand; play the Club King and Queen, pitching two Spades from dummy. Now lead the Spade Ace and follow with another Spade. The opponent who wins will shoot back another trump which you win in your hand (overtaking dummy's Queen with the Ace) to play your last Spade and ruff with dummy's last Heart. Come to your hand with the Diamond Ace and then, after all this, draw that last trump.

III. Suit Establishment

(1) With seven sure tricks West needs two more. He has eight Clubs; the opponents have five, which usually split 3-2, so Clubs probably will produce two extra tricks. Give up two rounds, then win the Ace.

(2) West has 11 tricks and needs one more. Try to establish a Diamond, which you can do if the outstanding six are divided 4-2 or 3-3. You have to play the suit five times, so you need five entries. Three will come from the suit itself. Duck a round, then the 6 to the Ace, and a Diamond back, ruffing high. The other two entries will be the Club Queen and the Club 8. Be careful to hold onto your Club 4 to cross over to dummy's 8.

(3) Possible additional winners are: in Spades, finessing for the Queen; in Diamonds, establishing a little Diamond; and in Clubs, establishing two small Clubs. Developing Clubs is superior. Declarer has eight, the opponents five. If those five split 3-2, the slam is cold. Duck a

Club, then win the Ace-King. If Clubs fail to break, fall back on the Diamond play. If the suit doesn't fall, as a last resort finesse the Spade.

(4) He can try to establish a little Diamond. He'll have to lead the suit five times. The suit itself will provide two rounds and East has three entries in trumps. He plays the Diamond Ace and ruffs a Diamond; a trump to the 9, and a Diamond back and ruffs high; a trump to the Jack, and a Diamond back and ruffs high. Now a trump to the Queen lands him in dummy to reach the Diamond 6 and discard the Heart loser.

IV. Dangerous Opponent

(1) Hold back the Club Ace until the third round. North, with two established winners, is the Dangerous Opponent. Lead the Diamond King, then the 9 and finesse. If the finesse fails and South wins the Queen, the contract is assured because South has no Clubs. South will probably return a Heart. Run up with the Ace and cash all winners, taking three Spades, four Diamonds, one Club, and one Heart.

(2) (a) When the Spade King won the first trick, North was known to hold the Ace. Therefore, South is the Dangerous Opponent because South can lead through the Q-7 of Spades. North is safe; if he leads a Spade declarer has a stop.

(b) Yes. There are eight top tricks consisting of one Heart, three Diamonds, three Clubs, and one Spade. To guarantee the contract, lead the Diamond 4 from dummy and finesse the 9. If this loses to North, you have five Diamond winners so you'll make an overtrick.

If the Diamond 9 wins, that's the ninth trick. Even if Diamonds are 5-0 the contract rolls.

(3) (a) South is the danger hand because he can lead a Diamond through the King.

(b) Yes, by transferring a loser. Give North trick one, discarding a Club! Win any return, draw trumps, lead to the Club Ace and then lead the Club Queen. If South covers, ruff, enter dummy with a trump and discard two Diamonds on the J-10 of Clubs.

If South doesn't cover, discard a Diamond. If North wins the Club King declarer still has 10 tricks, losing the Heart King, Club King, and Diamond Ace. If the opponents don't grab the Diamond Ace quickly, declarer gets two more pitches on Clubs and takes 11 tricks.

(4) (a) South is the Dangerous Opponent because he can make a damaging lead through the Heart King. If you lose two Hearts and the trump Queen you're dead.

(b) The contract is certain except in the unlikely circumstance that South holds all five outstanding trumps. Finesse trumps so only North can win. Take the Diamond King. If North follows you are home free. Then play the Jack and finesse. Assuming this loses to North, which is the worst that can happen, North is stymied because he can't profitably lead a Heart. Win any return, probably a Spade, pull the last trump. Run five Club tricks and discard Hearts. You take 11 tricks, losing a trump and a Spade at the end.

If South has the Diamond Queen, you make 12 tricks!

The trap to avoid is ruffing a Spade in dummy because you need dummy's trumps for repeated Diamond finesses in the event South holds Q-x-x-x.

V. Safety Plays

(1) You see 12 tricks — six Spades, three Clubs, a Club ruff, and two red Aces. It looks so e-a-s-y. Can any calamity befall you? Only if you lose one of your winners.

North's preempt indicates an eight-card suit. Playing the Heart Ace at trick one could jeopardize your contract. Even if East doesn't trump, there is no advantage to playing it. The duck guarantees the slam. Let North win. When he continues another Heart, you ruff and pull trumps. Later when All Is Quiet on the Western Front you cash the Heart Ace to discard the losing Diamond.

(2) Win the Club Ace, play the Ace-King-Queen of Spades, dropping the rest of the Clubs in the West hand, then start after trumps. Since you can afford to lose one trump, make the safety play. First play the King, then lead a small Heart toward dummy. If North plays low, finesse the 8. If this loses to South the suit is breaking 3-2 and

there are no more problems. If South shows out, the 8 wins. Cash the Ace, holding your losses to one trick. If North happens to show out, rise with the Ace and play through South's Q-10 toward your J-9-7, again holding yourself to one loser.

(3) There are no losers in the master hand unless the four trumps outstanding, J-7-4-3, are bunched in one hand. First, lay down the Queen. If both follow you won't lose any Spades.

If South shows out, lead the 10 and finesse North for the Jack. This brings in the whole suit.

If North shows out on the first round, next win the King on the board and take the marked finesse of South's J-7 on the way back to the A-10-9-8.

The play to avoid is first cashing the King, the honor in the hand with only one honor. You are then helpless if North started with four trumps.

(4) Outside the trump suit declarer has only two losers, so he can afford to lose one trump but not two. He takes the safety play. First, he lays down the Spade Ace. If an honor appears — the King or the Jack — the problem is solved. If no honor appears, he crosses to dummy (via the Heart Ace) to lead toward the Q-10. If the King pops up of course he plays low. If anything lower, he covers. If South holds K-J-x, declarer loses but one trick. If North holds K-J-x, declarer loses two tricks no matter how he plays the suit.

The play of the Ace protects against a singleton King in the North hand and also against a doubleton K-J.

VI. Counting

(1) In the auction North showed at least five Spades and five Hearts. When he followed to two rounds of Diamonds, twelve of his cards were known. He has either one Club or none.

The contract is guaranteed. Play the Club Ace first. If North doesn't drop the Queen, South has it. Lead a Club from dummy and finesse the 10 with confidence. Give up a Heart; win any return. Ruff a Heart to reach dummy and lead another Club, finessing the Jack.

You take five trump tricks, two ruffs in dummy and four Clubs. Total, eleven.

(2) West's rebid shows 19 to 20 points and East's bidding shows 7 to 11. With more he would make a slam try. That leaves somewhere between 9 and 13 for your partner.

With no entries, it's useless to try to set up your Clubs. Besides, declarer bid Clubs. It's better to try to hit partner. On this auction partner has four Spades or more. (Declarer has fewer than four Spades since he failed to bid Spades after East bid Hearts. East could have four Spades but not more.)

Lead the Spade 9 because partner's longest suit probably is Spades.

(3) The location of the 40 points in the deck is revealed. You and dummy have 21 points. South's No Trump overcall showed a minimum of 16; then North showed up with the Club King. That pinpoints the 19 points outstanding. South's hand is an open book; he began with three Kings, the A-Q of Clubs, and the Jack of Spades.

You will take ten tricks — five Hearts, one Spade, and four Diamonds.

Rise with the Spade Ace; lay down the trump Ace. If both opponents follow, don't bother to lead trumps anymore. Play the Diamond Queen and finesse. It is going to win. Then the Diamond Jack. South will cover this one and you take the Ace. Then give up a trick to the trump King and claim the rest.

VII. Endplays

(1) Yes! Win the Club Ace, take out trumps in one round, play the Diamond Ace and ruff a Diamond, ruff a Club, ruff a Diamond, and ruff a Club. This eliminates Clubs and Diamonds from the North-South hands. Cross to dummy with a trump, lead a Spade from dummy and insert the 10. West has to return a Spade for a free finesse. If he returns a Diamond or a Club, declarer trumps in dummy as he discards a Spade from his hand.

(2) You have two sure Spade losers and a Heart guess. If you could get an opponent to lead Hearts you'd eliminate the guess and be sure to win 11 tricks. You can

execute an endplay. Win the Spade Ace, pull trumps, cash the Club Ace and ruff a Club, cross to dummy with a trump and ruff a second Club. This eliminates Clubs.

Now give the opponents their two Spades. Then, whoever is on lead has to play Hearts, giving you a free finesse or according you a ruff and a sluff. Either way you have 11 tricks.

(3) Declarer has eleven tricks off the top. If the Clubs are divided, he can win his twelfth trick with a small Club; or, if East holds the Spade King, he can finesse and win the Queen.

On to the play. Win the Club Queen, then the Club King. This reveals West began with four Clubs. Take four Heart tricks eliminating Hearts from the deck. Take three Diamonds. On the third West cannot follow. Now take your other Club trick; give West his Club trick and he is endplayed. With no Hearts or Diamonds in his hand, he has to lead a Spade into your Ace-Queen and the contract is assured. There is nothing West can do to rescue himself from the endplay.

VIII. Squeezes

(1)

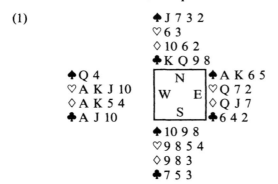

```
                    ♠ J 7 3 2
                    ♡ 6 3
                    ◊ 10 6 2
                    ♣ K Q 9 8
  ♠ Q 4                        ♠ A K 6 5
  ♡ A K J 10      N            ♡ Q 7 2
  ◊ A K 5 4    W     E         ◊ Q J 7
  ♣ A J 10        S            ♣ 6 4 2
                    ♠ 10 9 8
                    ♡ 9 8 5 4
                    ◊ 9 8 3
                    ♣ 7 5 3
```

West has 12 tricks and has that all-but-one-winner situation where he should think about a squeeze. If North, who undoubtedly has the Club Queen, also holds four Spades, he is busy in two suits and can be squeezed out of a vital card. He has to keep five cards and can't do it.

Declarer wins the Club Ace and cashes four Hearts and four Diamonds. On the ninth winner, North has to cut down to four cards. If he throws a Spade, declarer can win a small Spade for his thirteenth trick. If he throws the Club Queen, the Club Jack is turned into a winner.

(2)

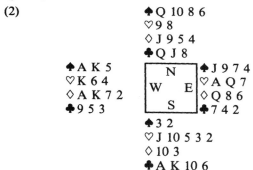

```
              ♠ Q 10 8 6
              ♡ 9 8
              ◊ J 9 5 4
              ♣ Q J 8
   ♠ A K 5      N      ♠ J 9 7 4
   ♡ K 6 4   W     E   ♡ A Q 7
   ◊ A K 7 2           ◊ Q 8 6
   ♣ 9 5 3      S      ♣ 7 4 2
              ♠ 3 2
              ♡ J 10 5 3 2
              ◊ 10 3
              ♣ A K 10 6
```

Yes, North can be squeezed. At this point declarer has eight winners and one loser. He first runs his Hearts and on the third Heart winner — the seventh trick — North has to discard down to six cards and no longer can keep three Spades and four Diamonds. If he throws a Diamond, declarer's small Diamond will be established. If he throws a Spade, declarer's Ace-King will fell the Queen, and dummy's Jack will become a winner.

On the fourth Club declarer should discard a Heart from his hand and a Diamond from dummy. On the third round of Hearts declarer has to make another pitch from his hand and he can afford a Spade. (The entry to dummy's Spade threat will be the Diamond Queen.)

(3)

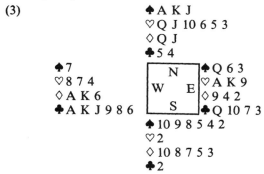

```
              ♠ A K J
              ♡ Q J 10 6 5 3
              ◊ Q J
              ♣ 5 4
   ♠ 7          N      ♠ Q 6 3
   ♡ 8 7 4   W     E   ♡ A K 9
   ◊ A K 6            ◊ 9 4 2
   ♣ A K J 9 8 6  S   ♣ Q 10 7 3
              ♠ 10 9 8 5 4 2
              ♡ 2
              ◊ 10 8 7 5 3
              ♣ 2
```

Declarer has 10 tricks and needs one more. His only chance is a squeeze.

North wins the Spade King and then plays the Heart Queen which dummy wins with the King. Now declarer pulls trumps. Next, he must correct the count. He has two losers so he must get rid of one if he is to manipulate a squeeze. He plays the Ace-King of Diamonds, then another Diamond. South wins. The defenders have their book. South shoots back a Spade and declarer ruffs.

Declarer has two threat cards, dummy's Spade Queen and dummy's Heart 9. Convinced North is busy in both suits, he runs all his Clubs. When the last trump is played at the eleventh trick, North has to discard before dummy and is down to the Spade King and the Heart J-10. If he throws the King of Spades, he sets up dummy's Queen; if he throws a Heart, dummy's King and 9 take the last two tricks.

IX. Reading the Dummy

(1)

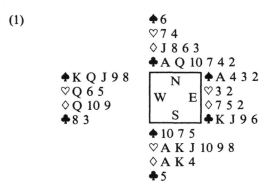

```
                    ♠ 6
                    ♡ 7 4
                    ◇ J 8 6 3
                    ♣ A Q 10 7 4 2
   ♠ K Q J 9 8         N         ♠ A 4 3 2
   ♡ Q 6 5        W       E      ♡ 3 2
   ◇ Q 10 9           S          ◇ 7 5 2
   ♣ 8 3                         ♣ K J 9 6
                    ♠ 10 7 5
                    ♡ A K J 10 9 8
                    ◇ A K 4
                    ♣ 5
```

Dummy says, "Go for an active defense." **Thought 1:** declarer can't run dummy's long Clubs because all the finesses are going to fail. **Thought 2:** declarer is going to want to ruff Spades. Since West might be embarrassed to lead a trump, East overtakes partner's Spade King with the

Ace to lead a Heart. Now declarer can ruff only one Spade so he is down one and East is a hero.

(2)

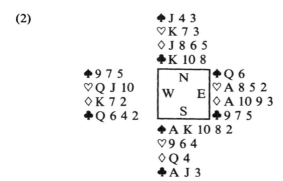

               ♠ J 4 3
               ♡ K 7 3
               ◇ J 8 6 5
               ♣ K 10 8

♠ 9 7 5   ♠ Q 6
♡ Q J 10   ♡ A 8 5 2
◇ K 7 2   ◇ A 10 9 3
♣ Q 6 4 2   ♣ 9 7 5

               ♠ A K 10 8 2
               ♡ 9 6 4
               ◇ Q 4
               ♣ A J 3

Dummy says, "Passive defense!" Dummy has no long suit to run and no apparent ruffing power, so West should pull back into his shell and let declarer break the suits. West should exit with a trump.

Declarer pulls trumps, winding up in dummy, and now has to open up the Diamond suit. He leads the 5, East plays low, declarer rises with the Queen, West wins the King and exits with the Diamond 7. Dummy covers with the 8 and East wins the 9. East gets out with his last Heart, declarer ruffing. Now declarer has to make the Club guess. If he misguesses, he goes down.

At trick four if West leads a Diamond or a Club, he sets up a trick for declarer and South coasts in with his contract.

(3)   West sees all dummy's Diamonds are coming in and declarer is going to get to discard a loser. So West adopts an active defense. He has one trick and needs three more. East's Club deuce said he didn't want a Club lead, so the Spade suit is the only hope. But naturally the problem isn't that easy! It has to be the Spade Queen!

Here's the layout:

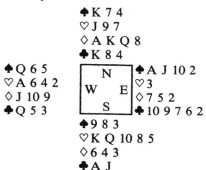

```
              ♠ K 7 4
              ♡ J 9 7
              ◇ A K Q 8
              ♣ K 8 4
♠ Q 6 5        ┌───────┐      ♠ A J 10 2
♡ A 6 4 2      │   N   │      ♡ 3
◇ J 10 9       │ W   E │      ◇ 7 5 2
♣ Q 5 3        │   S   │      ♣ 10 9 7 6 2
              └───────┘
              ♠ 9 8 3
              ♡ K Q 10 8 5
              ◇ 6 4 3
              ♣ A J
```

If West simply leads a low Spade, declarer plays low from dummy, and East can win the 10. However, with no means of getting West on lead for another Spade through, all East can do is cash the Ace and hold declarer to ten tricks.

West's reasoning might go this way: If partner has the A-x-x-x of Spades, the defense can get only one Spade trick. If East has A-J-x, the defense can get only two because declarer's 10 sets up. If East happens to hold A-J-10, the defense can garner three tricks if West forces the King by playing the Queen. Laying down the Queen in this instance makes all the difference in the world.

(4) At trick four West leads the Spade 3, in effect asking East to uppercut with his highest Heart. The whole hand is:

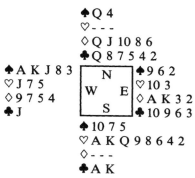

```
              ♠ Q 4
              ♡ - - -
              ◇ Q J 10 8 6
              ♣ Q 8 7 5 4 2
♠ A K J 8 3    ┌───────┐      ♠ 9 6 2
♡ J 7 5        │   N   │      ♡ 10 3
◇ 9 7 5 4      │ W   E │      ◇ A K 3 2
♣ J            │   S   │      ♣ 10 9 6 3
              └───────┘
              ♠ 10 7 5
              ♡ A K Q 9 8 6 4 2
              ◇ - - -
              ♣ A K
```

If East obliges by trumping with the 10, he forces an honor from South. Declarer now must lose a trump and go down one. If East trumps with the 3, South overruffs with the 4 and has no problem.

X. Negative Double

(1) (a) Double, negative. Don't raise Diamonds. First try to play a Heart contract. If partner rebids 2 Hearts, pass. You've already bid your hand. If partner bids 2 Clubs, then bid 2 Diamonds.

(b) You have an opening hand facing an opening hand; there's probably a game around, but you want to keep the auction low while you look for the best trump suit. Use the negative double to see if partner has four Hearts. If he says 2 Hearts, you'll jump to 4 Hearts. If he rebids Diamonds or bids Clubs, you'll jump to game in Diamonds. Your hand values at 16 and partner should be able to bring in eleven tricks.

(c) Pass. You don't have the points for a negative double that might drag poor South into 2 Hearts or 2 Diamonds.

(d) Use the negative double. You have a long Heart suit but not enough points to enter the auction at the 2-level. If partner rebids Diamonds or bids Clubs, you'll say 2 Hearts.

(2) (a) Double, asking partner to bid Spades if he has four of them.

(b) There's probably a game somewhere, maybe at 5 Clubs, but first see if you can play it in the more economical contract of 4 Spades. Utilize the negative double.

(c) Pass and pray partner will reopen with a double. Then you can pass, converting it to a penalty double.

(d) Bid 1 Spade, promising a five-card suit. Partner can now raise you with only three Spades.

(3) (a) Double, showing four cards in each major.

(b) 1 Spade to show five cards. You may get a chance to show the Hearts later, but it's imperative to get the Spade message across.

(4) (a) Bid 2 Hearts, showing four Hearts and a minimum opener of 13-15.

(b) Jump to 4 Hearts, showing a Heart fit and 19-21 opener.

(c) Bid 1 No Trump. Don't worry about Hearts. Partner has four Hearts and at least 6 points. Some of them are probably in Hearts. You have a minimum opener so make a minimum rebid.

(d) Jump to 3 Hearts to show the Heart fit and a medium opener.